You Win Some . . .

You Lose Some

Recollections of a Newfoundland Fishery Officer

William Roche

You Win Some . . .

You Lose Some

Recollections of a Newfoundland Fishery Officer

William Roche

CREATIVE PUBLISHERS

St. John's, Newfoundland
2002

Le Conseil des Arts | The Canada Council
du Canada | for the Arts

We acknowledge the support of The Canada Council for the Arts for our
publishing program.

We acknowledge the financial support of the Government of Canada through the Book
Publishing Industry Development Program (BPIDP) for our publishing program.

Cover photo of Fish Cove on Bull Point in Point Lance

∞ Printed on acid-free paper

Published by
CREATIVE BOOK PUBLISHING
a division of 10366 Newfoundland Limited
a Robinson-Blackmore Printing & Publishing associated company
P.O. Box 8660, St. John's, Newfoundland A1B 3T7

Printed in Canada by:
ROBINSON-BLACKMORE PRINTING & PUBLISHING

National Library of Canada Cataloguing in Publication

Roche, William, 1938-
        You win some-- you lose some : recollections of a Newfoundland
fishery officer / William Roche.

ISBN 1-894294-45-9

        1. Roche, William, 1938-. 2. Canada. Dept. of Fisheries and
Oceans--Anecdotes. 3. Fishery conservation--Newfoundland--Anecdotes. I. Title.

SH224.N7R63 2002   639.2'2'09718   C2002-902833-7

Dedicated
to Derek Rolls
a deceased
friend and a fellow
Fishery Officer

CONTENTS

ABOUT THE AUTHOR

William E. (Billy) Roche was born in Branch, St. Mary's Bay, Newfoundland in 1938. As a young man, he joined the Royal Canadian Navy in the Weapons Underwater Department. He then took an honourable discharge after his hitch was served in 1965.

He went to work at construction and as a heavy equipment operator for the next couple of years, until he began his career with the Department of Fisheries and Oceans as a Fishery Officer, Conservation and Protection in 1971. With his headquarters in Branch, he began his work which consisted of patrols of both coastal and inland waters.

In addition to his fishery officer duties, he became an Auxiliary Member of the Royal Canadian Mounted Police, from 1975 to 1981, until he was forced to leave when the stress and workload became too demanding.

He also served as Chief of the Branch Volunteer Fire Department for fifteen years during the 1970's and 1980's. For his service, he was appointed by the Minister of Justice as Assistant to the Fire Commission. In addition, he was a member of numerous other organizations throughout the Parish and local area.

In 1992, he was presented with the Gunter Behr Award, as officer of the year, Conservation and Protection. He retired in May, 1995.

ACKNOWLEDGEMENTS

I would like to thank the following people who encouraged and assisted in the writing and publication of this book: my niece Kim Careen who told me I could and should write this book; a good friend of mine, Anthony Lundrigan, who likewise encouraged me to write a book of stories about my career; my niece Emily and nephew Peter Roche who assisted in the editing and typing of the book; and finally to Rick Peacock and my nephew Don Nash for the marvelous photos found throughout.

Special thanks also go to Dawn Roche and Dwayne LaFitte of Creative Book Publishing for agreeing to publish my manuscript.

Count One
for the Warden

Cat and Mouse Game in Placentia Bay

For many years Department of Fisheries and Oceans (DFO) Officers and personnel got many complaints from Placentia Bay fishermen who return to the Islands to fish for lobster, cod, etc. Most of them had left their lobster pots at their fishing premises or along coves close to their traditional fishing areas. The same was done with gillnets and other equipment stored in their sheds as it would create a real hardship for them to return all the fishing gear to their community of residence. The problem with all this was the poachers. They would go out to these isolated areas in the late fall, after most fishing had ended for the season, and set some of these pots and nets back in the water to poach cod and lobster.

Many patrols were carried out by officers such as myself in search of such illegal fishing. However, with many miles of shoreline, and with maybe only a floating nylon rope attached to the net or pot, it was difficult to find them unless you had specific information on their locations; or plain good luck. Occasionally we were successful, but in most cases the poachers had the last say.

In the fall of 1993, I got a specific complaint from a longliner crew who had gone over to Presque along with family members who had once lived there. On their journey, they became aware of a longliner type boat called the *William E.* and noted its suspicious actions. In one case, they actually saw what appeared to be a crate of lobsters being hauled on board as they approached the same wharf. The *William E.* then departed the area as the other boat came alongside. I gathered all the information that I could on the matter and sent it up to my supervisors in Grand Bank as I suspected the boat was from that area. Apparently the officers at Grand Bank were familiar with this vessel and crew as similar complaints had been previously received.

Officer Ken Durdle, our sub-district supervisor, personally took on the investigation of taking statements from the visiting longliner crew as well the suspects from the *William E.* However, due to the lack of evidence from the complainants and the denial by the suspects, it was decided that there wasn't enough to warrant charges for illegal fishing. However, a determination was made to give this particular boat and crew close scrutiny next fall.

Officer Onslow Brenton was assigned the task of making arrangements to keep abreast of *William E.*'s movements in the fall of 1994. It was on Saturday, November 12th when I got a call from Officer Derek Rolls instructing that we were to leave Placentia at 2 a.m. that night, go on board the Fishery Patrol boat at Arnold's Cove and pick up food supplies enough to last six people for a few days. From Arnold's Cove we continued on to Swift Current where we met Officers Brenton, Ryan, Slaney and Sheppard. They had with them two speed boats and after launching and putting all our supplies on board, we left Swift Current around 5 a.m. With skilled helmsman, and everyone peering into the darkness, we managed to escape the

4

many rocks and shoals in that particular part of Swift Current Harbour.

We were on our way to St. Leonard's and Presque to search for the *William E.* when we realized that we must must be careful and spot them before they spotted us. Information gathered concluded that the vessel and crew did most of the poaching in the Presque, Clattice Harbour areas using a speed boat and using Toslow as their anchoring place.

Fishery Officer Slaney and I landed in St. Leonard's as I had previous experience of walking the trails in that area. We walked over to St. Kyran's and using our binoculars, scanned Presque Harbour. There was no sign of the suspect boats. Calling back on radio, we informed the others who had also peeked into Isle-a-Valen that there was no boat of any kind. Our fellow officers in the two boats then continued on to our location in Presque.

We then made the decision that Officers Brenton, Ryan and Sheppard would attempt to walk over to Clattice Harbour, if the trail wasn't totally grown in. Securing the boats in a cove inside the government wharf at St. Kyran's, they began their hike. They returned a few hours later to say that they had arrived just in time to see the *William E.* leave Clattice Harbour. Furthermore, in checking on a fishing premises in the area, they found freshly baited and wet lobster pots that apparently had been removed from the water that day. It was obvious that their intention was not to return to Clattice Harbour anytime in the near future. Now what were the officers to do?

Officer Brenton, being in charge, decided that Fishery Officer Ryan and I were to go over to Merasheen Island and from there monitor the shoreline from Isle-A-Valen to Toslow. The others would remain in Presque in case the suspects doubled-back. Officers were landed at a couple of sites close to the harbour entrance while the others remained with the boat. It didn't take Officer Ryan and I long to get to Merasheen and by 3 p.m. we saw the suspect longliner steaming up towards Toslow.

Along the way she stopped, and for an hour or so, appeared to be either hauling gillnets or jigging. Due to the distance involved, it was difficult to be sure. As evening shadows began to close, the *William E.* entered Toslow Harbour. We made radio contact with the others, and feeling confident we were now in a better situation to resume our surveillance of the suspect vessel, we returned to the fishery cabin at Best's Harbour.

Leaving Best's Harbour at 6 a.m., we proceeded on to St. Leonard's. Upon arrival, Officer Slaney and I again landed and walked over to St. Kyran's. No boat there! But wait! Way up at the other end of Presque Harbour in Beckford Cove a small boat could be seen moving around. Calling back to the other officers, we informed them that we believed the speedboat to be in Beckford Cove.

The decision was made that our officers would try and sneak in through Presque Harbour entrance and get some officers landed on an island there as well as in the St. Ann's area. This was done successfully without raising any alarm. While dropping off the officers, a scallop drag was spotted on one of the small islands and it had been recently used. We continued our surveillance, but by early afternoon, the suspects in the speedboat spotted one of our boats. It was obvious that they were taking no chances and they returned to Beckford Cove. As our boats had no DFO markings, and officers were in survival suits, we felt we still had a chance to surprise them.

After an hour or so, the suspects hauled their boat ashore at Beckford and disappeared into the trees. One was still wearing his survival suit. Through radio communication we decided that they may very well be walking back to Toslow to join the *William E*. All landed, the officers were picked up by our boats and we headed for Toslow as we knew we would get there before the three suspects.

Arriving at Toslow mid afternoon, we spotted the *William E*. Boarding the boat, it was soon determined that nobody was on board. The door to the wheel house was locked and the fish hold was empty. Peering in through a window in the wheelhouse, we could see a couple of buckets with fillets in them, as well a couple of boxes of cod, lots of fresh blood and bloody knives. A recent filleting operation had taken place here. One of the officers then spotted a green net bag in close to the shoreline. Upon closer inspection it showed to contain twenty-seven lobsters. We were convinced that there was enough evidence on board this vessel to warrant further surveillance.

Officer Rolls, being a Lieutenant in the Canadian Rangers, had brought along some camouflage gear as well as face paint to blend in with the surroundings. Applying the gear, he and Officer Sheppard were landed on the south side of the harbour to monitor the *William E*. from the low forest vegetation and trees on the hillside. Myself and the other officers then left Toslow and proceeded a short distance up the shore-line and hid away in a small cove to await the arrival of the suspects.

About a hour later, we got a call on our radio from Officer Rolls that the three suspects had been spotted crawling around the trees on the opposite side of the Harbour. Through constant radio contact we were kept abreast of the Cat and Mouse game unfolding in Toslow. Officer Rolls, in a low voice, would tell us of their sneaking around, and at times, looking exactly in their direction but failing to spot them due to their camouflage faces and clothes.

As the afternoon was wearing on, we had a discussion amongst the four of us in the boats. What were we to do next? Wait till they went on board the *William E.* or move now and search the boat? I suggested to Officer Brenton that the guy wearing the survival suit most likely had a reason for not leaving it behind as the other two had done. The reason may well be that he intended to swim out to the *William E.* at dark as she was anchored only a hundred feet or so from the shoreline. Once on board and in a matter of minutes, the fillets and cod could be dumped over the side. As for the lobsters, we could not prove at this time a connection with the suspects. Also once the fish was dumped, it would complicate things for us in court in proving ownership.

Officer Brenton made the decision to move now as we still had a half hour or so of daylight. In a matter of minutes, the four of us steamed into Toslow. By this time the two officers on land had made contact with the suspects and all were waiting for us on shore.

Officer Brenton informed them of our surveillance for the past two days and proceeded to read them their rights. They acknowledged that they understood and after identifying all three suspects, we proceeded to board the *William E.* Two officers were also dispatched to get the bag of lobsters.

About ninety pounds of cod fillets and about fifty pounds of round cod was found; as well twenty-two cod heads. All items were considered illegal as the accused had no fishing licenses.

In a private conversation between all fishery officers, we decided that seizure of the vessel would not take place at this time but rather later after she had reached home port. Satisfied that we had accomplished our goal concerning this particular vessel and crew, we released twenty-six of the twenty-seven lobsters and departed Toslow for our cabin at Best's Harbour. Once again a hearty meal was cooked up, and all being tired, turned in for a good night's sleep.

The following morning, the wind was strong from the south and it was raining. I personally wasn't in favour of crossing the open water in this weather, but the decision was made to head back to Swift Current.

On the way back to Placentia, Fishery Officer Rolls and I stopped off at the fish plant at Arnold's Cove and sold eighty pounds of cod fillets and fifty pounds of round cod, keeping a sample of each as evidence including the cod heads which the plant manager wasn't interested in buying. All items were sold in the name of the Receiver General of Canada and the items kept for evidence were tagged and froze at our Placentia office.

On November 21, the officers from Grand Bank seized the vessel *William E.* She was consequently towed by our Fishery Patrol boat to Fortune where she was taken from the water and secured at the haul-out until a final decision was made by the courts.

After all the paper work was completed; reports to supervisors, court and appearance documentation etc., trial was set for April 3, 1995. Although our evidence was consistent, it also lacked certain positives, such as who caught the lobsters? The mother of one of the accused pleaded with us to go easy on her son as a conviction would mean the loss of his job.

Two of the three pleaded guilty and received a fine of $5,000 each. The charges against the third individual were withdrawn at our request. The vessel *William E.* was returned to the owner by order of the court. Just another of the thousands of stories from Placentia Bay.

Double Back

It was capelin time and the commercial fishery was in full swing. As a result, I had been assigned to work on the Fishery Patrol boat *Groswater Bay* to carry out patrols in Placentia Bay and the Cape St. Mary's area.

Landing at Argentia, I managed to contact Fishery Guardians Don Nash and John O'Rourke and together we started out the Cape Shore towards our headquarters in Branch. As we drove through the community of Cuslett, I noticed some pieces of heavy equipment down on the beach. Upon checking things out, we saw a contractor with an overhead loader and two large trucks loading sand and beach gravel from the low tide area. This being illegal at any time of the year was especially serious at this particular period as the capelin were spawning on these very beaches. Getting out of the fishery vehicle, I went over and spoke with the loader operator and explained to him that this was illegal. He indicated to me that he wasn't aware of his law-breaking and how he was only following orders from his boss who was not present. I also informed the drivers of the dump trucks of the situation. They were to immediately stop removing the beach and, failure to do so, may result in seizure of the machines as well as charges laid against them. They agreed to do so right away and would explain my instructions to their boss. Getting back aboard the truck, we continued our journey back towards our headquarters.

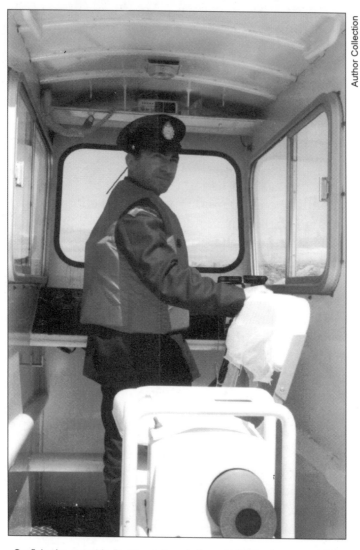

Author Collection

On fisheries patrol in St. Mary's Bay during mid 1970s. Accompanied by Constable Rick Peacock of RCMP who is not shown.

About four miles down the road, I asked Don Nash, who was driving, to turn around and go back to the beach. I had a strange feeling that my instructions were being ignored, as I knew the contractor well.

Arriving back at the beach, we found the operation back in full swing. This time the boss was there who was also the owner of the machinery.

I again ordered the loader operator up from the beach and asked him why he had disobeyed my instructions. He said, "I take my orders from the boss who is now here." After checking the contents of both the large tandem trucks, I saw that they were loaded down with sand and beach. I even saw some capelin mixed in; some still alive.

By this time the owner of the machinery got out of his truck and came over to where I was talking to the loader operator, asking me what the problem was and why I had ordered them to stop the operation. I explained to him the laws governing the removal of sand and gravel from beaches during all seasons and especially now at this sensitive time when the capelin were spawning. I also asked him if the loader operator had given him my earlier instructions and reasons. He said "yes" but that this was their last load as they now had enough sand and beach to meet their requirements.

At this point I decided that I had heard enough to convince me that these guys weren't ignorant to what they had been doing but rather choose to ignore the laws as well as my warning and authority in this matter. I consequently read the owner of the machinery the police caution and informed him that he would be charged with illegally disrupting spawning beds.

At this point he became very angry and said that he would complete the loading and only then would he not return to the beach. He also said that if I made any attempt to seize his equipment, he would physically keep me from doing so.

At this point I called over to Fishery Guardians Nash and O'Rourke to assist me in placing the accused under arrest. The accused suddenly calmed down when he realized the seriousness of the situation and agreed to remove his machinery immediately. That is exactly what he did and we hung around for awhile later to ensure that the equipment had left the area. The accused was charged under the habitat regulation, re: disturbing spawning bed areas; as well he was also charged with obstructing an officer in the performance of his duty by returning to the beach after being instructed not to do so.

Later that fall, the accused was convicted in Judge Barnable's court at Placentia for habitat violation and fined. The second offence of obstruction was transferred to the courthouse at Harbour Grace and to a different judge. He was found guilty on that charge as well despite having an excellent defence attorney. Heavy fines were imposed for each charge and he was also given a year of probation.

Pea Brain

*I*t had been a very successful crab fishery in the area and all assigned quotas had been taken by the various boat sizes. As fishery officer, it was my responsibility to inform local fishermen that the crab fishery would close today at 6:00 p.m.

The following evening, I was sitting by my window, looking out at the traffic going to and fro, I noticed a large fish-hauling truck go out the road towards nearby communities. I knew the truck was empty by the speed on the uphill grade and glancing at the wall clock saw that it was just past 11:00 p.m. Now where is that truck and driver going this hour of night as there are no fish landings at this particular time? (The Moratorium had been called a year or two earlier and the crab season was now closed). This sighting bothered me to such an extent that I put on my uniform and jumped in the fishery vehicle to begin a search for the truck and driver.

Arriving at the nearest community around at 1:00 a.m., I drove down a winding narrow road towards the landing site of some local boats. About halfway out, I came face to face with the suspect truck. There was no choice only for both of us to stop. Getting out of my vehicle, I approached the truck and spoke with the driver. Being familiar with the driver and the fish company he worked for, we greeted each other and I went on to ask what he was doing out here at this hour of night. He seemed hesitant to answer, so I insisted that he open the back doors of the truck so I could check inside. When he opened the doors, I immediately saw about a ton of fresh crab less than twenty-four hours old.

I informed the driver of the offence and of his legal rights. He acknowledged that he understood and stated that he was only following instructions from his employer. About this time, I heard in the direction towards the landing site, the full throttle of an engine. No doubt it was the crab boat heading to sea without any running lights on.

I informed the driver to drive ahead of me to my office located in my home and upon arrival, I telephoned his boss—a senior manager in the compound and apprised him of the situation. He indicated he understood my seizing the crab, but why the company truck as they needed her on a daily basis. To this I replied, "If you will provide me with a forklift to off load the crab at your plant, the truck will be immediately released back to the company at that time." He agreed to have the machinery and an operator at his plant upon our arrival in a couple of hours.

Arriving at the fish plant around 4:00 a.m., just as promised, the forklift operator was waiting to off load the seized crab. The seizure was weighed in and I obtained a receipt from the company made out to the Receiver General of Canada and also told those present that the truck was now released from seizure as agreed with management.

The following afternoon, I returned to the fish plant to speak with the manager whom I had spoken with earlier that night. After waiting an hour or more, I was finally brought to the manager's office. I officially informed him who I was and went on to explain that the truck driver said, in his cautioned statement, that he was obeying his employer's instructions in picking up and transporting the illegal crab. Therefore, I asked him for a cautioned statement concerning the matter as he may have been party to the offence. I would like to say at this point that I had described the truck driver in my notebook as approximately 6'3", 250 pounds, muscular, etc. The manager sat back in his chair and in an agitated tone stated, "I got nothing to say at this time. Contact my lawyer if you have further questions on this matter. As for the truck driver, he's a big man but he's got a pea-sized brain." As I departed the office, I looked the manger in the eye and said, "It was my experience that the ones with the pea-sized brains were the fish managers and processors!"

Renew's Rock

*O*t was in August of 1982 that Fishery Officer Richard (Dick) Didham and I were instructed to carry out an undercover operation on the Southern Shore, in particular, the area around Renew's Rock.

At our briefing by Supervisor Bill Davis and Fishery Officer Bud Parsons, we were told of the numerous problems and complaints concerning the small but prolific fishing area around Renew's Rock. The fishermen from the local area had asked DFO to ban gillnets from a four square mile area around the rock, and to have a season for trawl fishing and a season for jigging. This was enforced but problems were still plaguing the locals as some fishermen refused to abide by the seasons and restrictions. The local fishery officers had a problem dealing with the matter as they were so well known and monitored. We were also informed that the trawl season inside this area had ended and jigging was only permitted, but that some individuals continued to set and take back trawls.

Dick and I proceeded in an unmarked vehicle up to the area, and during the night, managed to get an eighteen-foot aluminum boat and engine from the DFO shed. With only a compass for navigation, we proceeded to the restricted area around the rock and observed three or four boats fishing in what we thought to be the restricted area. Throwing a couple of lead weights over the side, we made it look as we too were trying to jig a few fish. It was easy to observe who was jigging as their movements differed from someone who was hauling a trawl.

As we slowly drifted closer to the boats, one boat with two occupants caught our attention, as both were in the bow of the boat and appeared to be hauling a trawl. This is what we were here for, and with that in mind, slowly made our way towards the suspects. As we got closer, they became more aware of us and went to working their jiggers that they had apparently placed over the side earlier.

Pulling up alongside the suspects' boat, I noticed a line going from the stem of the boat down into the water. Dick said to me, "That's the trawl!" and I agreed. With this in mind we then identified ourselves as fishery officers and asked them for identification, licenses, etc. After we had fully documented their fishing licenses and their identification, I asked what the line going from the stem of the boat down into the water was. They replied, "There's a strong tide today, so we put out our anchor." I therefore asked that they pull the anchor up for verification as both Officer Didham and I suspected it as being a trawl. At this disclosure they stated that they were outside the restricted area and as local fishermen knew the area well. They asked us how we could prove otherwise as Renew's Rock is not visible above water. We replied but stating that we had reasonable and probable grounds to believe they were illegally fishing with a trawl during closed season and it would be seized as evidence for further investigation. To this they replied "If the trawl is seized, then you guys are responsible for taking it in." They then said they were leaving to go back to port and we agreed that they may do so.

After the two had departed, Dick and I discussed the means of how we could prove we were inside the restricted area, as we had no way of determining longitude and latitude of our position. Having fished with my father during my teens, I often observed and discussed with him the marking of landmarks to determine where to set gear on shoals, rocks, etc. As the day was clear and sunny, we set about securing the trawl to our boat and looking around for landmarks. Looking in towards Cappahayden, I noticed a white bungalow, with a brown roof and an attached garage. The roof of the house was in a direct line with a very large boulder on a hill behind the house. Both of us made entries in our notebooks to this effect. To find two more stationary objects, we looked down towards Bear Cove Head and Port Kirwan. There we saw a lime coloured house off to itself in a field and this house was in a straight line with the bill of Bear Cove Head. We were satisfied that we could now determine the latitude and longitude at a later date. Now the hard part, taking back the trawl along with about three hundred pounds of cod. With blood and sweat, we managed.

Returning to Renews, the fish were sold to a local fish buyer and a receipt made out to the Receiver General. The seized trawl was secured in the DFO shed and we returned to the local fishery office to phone in our report to the district office and supervisor at St. John's.

Fishery Officer Bud Parsons answered my phone call and I proceeded to give him the details of our day and the name of the suspects, as well as the seizure and securing of the trawl and cod. Bud listened to all of this patiently and when I had concluded my report he said, "Billy, do you know who those two are?" I said,"Of course," as we had checked their I.D. "Yes," he said, "but do you know who they are related to?" To which I said, "What has that got to do with it?" He then proceeded to tell me that both of them were the brothers-in-law of one of our most senior managers for DFO in Newfoundland. "Well," I concluded, "that's how the cookie sometimes crumbles and let the crumbs fall where they may."

As one of our fishery patrol boats was tied up in St. John's at the time, arrangements were made to have the captain and crew steam up to Fermeuse the next day to pick up Officer Didham and myself. This was done and we proceeded to Renew's Rock. As the weather was again cooperating with us, it did not take us long to maneuver the patrol boat into position where our earlier landmarks aligned themselves. The captain charted the latitude and longitude and compared it with coordinates for the outer closed area. As it turned out, the two locals had indeed been fishing well inside the restricted area with trawls. We would now proceed with pressing charges against the two for trawl-fishing out of season.

Upon our return, Fishery Officer Didham and I proceeded with the required paperwork. Information and summons against the two accused was recorded, and a plea date was set for mid-September in the municipal building in Ferryland; presided by Magistrate Terry Corbett. A not guilty plea was entered by the defendant's lawyer; then one of the more capable and upcoming lawyers in the area. The case was set for October and one of the first to be called to the stand was the captain of the fishery patrol boat. In order to be considered by the court as an expert witness, he had to first establish his credentials. When the defence lawyer asked for his papers of competency, the captain replied that he had left them aboard his boat. The trial was then postponed until February.

In February 1983, we all came together again in the Ferryland court and the captain produced his papers of certification as a captain. Upon close examination of the papers on the part of the defence lawyer, he asked the captain if it was true that he had only a Grade Eight education. The captain replied "yes," and the lawyer smelling blood and acquittal for his clients, went after the captain without mercy questioning his competence as an expert witness (ie: determining the longitude and latitude of the set trawl). The captain kept his composure under the cruel and humiliating attempts by the defence lawyer. Magistrate Corbett intervened and stated that he had a few questions for the captain. The Magistrate wanted to know how long he had been a captain and where he had sailed his vessel. "Twenty-eight years," the captain replied, "and I sailed all along the coast of Newfoundland and Labrador, your honour." Magistrate Corbett subsequently wanted to know if the captain ever had a mishap with his vessel during his twenty-eight years to which the captain replied, "No, your honour, I never chipped the paint off my boat." To this the Magistrate stated that he was satisfied that the captain was an expert witness.

Officer Didham and I were also called to the stand and quizzed on how we came about determining land marks and consequently determining the longitude and latitude of the trawls. I recalled in my evidence that cross referencing landmarks was considered as one of the most reliable means of knowing where shoals, rocks, etc. were located by our forefathers. The

Magistrate agreed and a conviction was rendered—
guilty as charged. A considerable fine on the two
accused was imposed.

The Sheathed Knife

*F*ederal fishery officers are responsible for conserving and protecting, not only the commercial fishery, but the inland/sport fishery as well. It is therefore, vitally important to have good, qualified fishery guardians to work with. I was exceptionally fortunate in this matter as the two Guardians that worked with me right up until my retirement were fantastic—John O'Rourke and Don Nash. In addition to being totally dedicated, they were professional as well.

It was July and John was on patrol in the Falls areas of Branch River. At the upper pool of the Falls, he came upon a poacher well known to us all, and he was at it again—jigging salmon from the pool. Being the professional that he is, Johnny informed the poacher of his rights and seized the rod and salmon. In the process, he was verbally abused and threatened. This hardened poacher always carried an eight-inch knife at his side. After dealing professionally with the poacher, Johnny continued on further up the river on patrol. It's about an hour's walk from the Falls to the highway where the fishery's truck was parked. After completing his patrol, Johnny returned to the truck. Low and behold what should be facing him but four slashed tires and Mr. Poacher with the sheathed knife and with a grin on his face informing Johnny, "You got four flat tires." As we could not fully prove who

24

slashed the tires, we left it as it was except for a vow to keep an extra lookout for the man with the knife.

Photo courtesy of Don Nash

Fishery Guardian John O'Rourke on stakeout at Red Rock on Branch River.

A few years later, Johnny and Donnie were again

on patrol at the headwaters of Branch River, and living out of a small tent. Being late in the season, salmon were gathering at the headwaters in preparation for spawning. In the late afternoon, they heard the noise of an approaching ATV. They took up a vantage point from a concealed area and awaited the arrivals. "Well now," Johnny said, "It's the poacher with the knife."

The poacher lost no time in raking the pool with his favourite hook—a three-pronged jigger. Again, relying on past experiences and professional decision-making, the two maintained their observation point and took notes of the poacher's actions. The five basic W's in law enforcement are: Who, When, Where, What and Why.

Night slowly settled in and they returned to their tent knowing that at a pre-arranged time, I would be calling them on the radio to get an update on their safety. We made radio contact and they updated me on the day's events—giving a detailed account of the knife man and his actions. They also asked for further instructions. Being personally familiar with the knife man and of his past threats and behaviour towards wardens, I instructed Donnie and Johnny not to make contact with the poacher, but continue observing his movements and actions. I would, in the meantime, arrange to have a helicopter transport myself and an RCMP officer to the area to deal with the situation. After we all were in agreement, we signed off in preparation for the following morning's plans.

With a bright and clear morning, our plan was put into action. I drove to the RCMP detachment at Placentia and around 8:00 a.m. the police officer and I boarded the helicopter which had just arrived from St. John's and proceeded to the headwaters of Branch River.

During the ride in, I again called Johnny and Donnie to update them and to be updated. Yes, the knife man was still there, cooking breakfast and chatting with some new arrivals. So far, so good.

Arriving at the scene, we landed close to the salmon pool and the poacher's tent. Donnie and Johnny also made their presence known at this point. There were surprised looks on some people's faces by now. After the RCMP officer and I had privately talked with the guardians, away from the accused and other anglers, we approached the man with the sheathed knife. This being a fishery matter, I took the leading role. Approaching the poacher, I identified myself, even though we knew each other for years. I also informed him of what Johnny and Donnie had witnessed the previous evening and of his legal rights. Before the formalities were through, the man with the sheathed knife still prominently displayed on his hip, became very angry and abusive towards all present. It was at this time that the RCMP officer intervened and with his hand on his pistol informed the accused to control himself or face arrest. Realizing he was outmanned and with strong evidence presented of his previous evening's actions, he gave up.

After a brief statement was obtained by me as well as documentation of the accused, we proceeded to seize the 4x4 ATV, his fishing equipment and fish. They were all sent to the DFO storage garage and a trial date was set. Guilty as charged was registered by the court.

Mint Brook

*O*t was about the mid-eighties when our Chief of Conservation and Protection with DFO, Ernie Collins, called me into St. John's and asked if myself and Joshua Burdett, a fishery officer from Labrador, would be willing to go to the Gambo-Gander area to work in an undercover operation. There were serious reports of heavy salmon poaching on the area's rivers and brooks. Ernie said that he had chosen us because of our experience in inland and commercial patrols, and because of the fact that we would not be recognized by the people in the area. Josh and I agreed, and after being briefed by Ernie and his assistant Don Wells, we collected all necessary camping equipment, rented a vehicle and started out on our undercover operation. One of the things that came up in our briefing was that we should not break our cover for minor violations. Notes were to be made of such incidences, but it was important to hold our cover for netting operations.

As we drove along the TCH and nearing Mint Brook in Gambo, we observed a number of people peering down into a brook. One person in particular was on the outside of the rail, wearing dark glasses and clearly excited. I told Josh that before the week was out, we were going to know this person as a serious poacher. It was just something I sensed.

We continued on to Gander and checked in at a hotel. After supper, we took a drive down around Gambo to the Smallwood Park area; an area that we had been told in our briefing where quite a bit of poaching was taking place. The park was fairly crowded, as it was mid-July, so it was easy for us to blend in while walking around. In our excursion, we got to know the area fairly well and choose a likely netting area. As a result we planned a stakeout which we would set up for later that night. We also checked the area of the bridge and along Mint Brook Road heading inland to get familiar with that area as well.

At nightfall, we returned to the park and stopped at the location we had decided upon earlier. From there we walked to a pool that had a falls. It was an ideal place for salmon gathering in their effort to get over the barrier. We quickly settled in a cluster of small trees and made ourselves as comfortable as possible.

There were a few cabins just up the trail from our location and from the noise, it was easy to tell that they were having a party as lots of laughter and shouting filtered down to us.

12 a.m., 1 a.m., 2 a.m. passed. "Maybe the partying in the cabins was keeping the poachers away," I thought. At around 2:30 a.m. we heard voices and footsteps approaching us, and peering out into the night, we saw six to eight people passing us by with nothing but towels wrapped around themselves; the party people. Upon reaching the falls and the pool, the towels were removed and they all dove in. Boy, what a time to shine our flashlights. After a short dip, they returned to their towels and then back to their cabins. So much for our first night's patrol.

As the chances for netting salmon in inland waters are much greater in late evening or night, we returned to our hotel rooms for a hearty breakfast and a good sleep. That evening, we returned to Mint Brook and drove along a dirt road that parallels the brook for a couple of miles. We had spotted a narrow footpath leading to a series of three pools the evening before, and it was here where we decided to do our stakeout for the rest of the evening. As there were still a couple of hours of daylight, we selected a site overlooking all three pools.

As we began to settle in, we spotted a lone angler walking to the lower pool. It wasn't long after that we saw him nervously glance around before dipping his rod down into the pool up to his wrist, with only about two feet of line extended from his rod. With a quick jerk of the wrist he had a salmon hooked. This guy had done this before as the pool was very deep and he had to know just where the salmon lay to be this good. While Josh and I were making notes of the time, date, place and physical description of the man and his actions, two more salmon were quickly jigged in the same manner. He then proceeded to clean the salmon and walked back up the trail out of sight. We remained at this location until nightfall and then drove to the brook in the park and settled down for the night beside a pool just above the highway.

During the night, we had two visits by three people to the brook. Overhearing part of their conversation, where they mentioned a vehicle, our vehicle, parked not too far away, they were too professional and cautious to try anything. Another daybreak, and still no netters; but a lesson learned about parking the vehicles too close to the pool. Again, we returned to our room for some sleep.

That evening, we went back to the three pools on Mint Brook and settled down a bit closer to the lower pool. It wasn't long before we spotted the same guy who had jigged three salmon the evening before. However, this time he was accompanied by two young boys.

Demonstrating his method of jigging to the young boys, he soon had another fish hooked. The boys cleaned it while he proceeded to jig two more. Josh and I began our approach while they were still busy cleaning the salmon. I said to Josh "Go along with me on this, I'm going to try something out-of-the-ordinary." We approached the man and the boys and got to talking about the good salmon fishing in the brook. During the conversation, we found out that the man and his two sons were from the Gambo area. As they were about to depart, I decided to make the move that I had been planning since we had first seen him. Taking out my badge and I.D., with Josh doing the same, we identified ourselves as fishery officers and told him about being witnesses to him jigging the three salmon; as well as the three he had jigged the evening before. It was at this point that I made my pitch and said, "Sir, you are a professional poacher and you are also ensuring that your sons grow up to be the same. With the evidence we have against you, plus the fact that you are encouraging and teaching your young sons to do the same thing, we can pretty much guarantee you that the judge will deal with you most severely, especially for what you are teaching your sons." At this time, he instructed his sons to wait for him by the truck. After they departed he said, "Sir, I don't want that to happen. Is there any way out of this for me and my sons?" This was just what we wanted to hear and said "As a resident of Gambo, you must know all the big time poachers in the area." "Yes, I do," he said. "Well then," I instructed, "here's something for you to think about. Tomorrow afternoon meet us up at the dump site with the names and descriptions of the people and vehicles as well as their areas of poaching and we will put this matter of the past two evenings on hold. If your information is good, we'll write you a warning ticket for letting your fly sink while angling for salmon. Fail to meet us tomorrow afternoon and we will be at your door with a summons as we all know each other now."

After the man departed to join his sons, Josh and I decided to drive further in the gravel road so as to better acquaint ourselves with the area in case we needed to do another stakeout. What we failed to realize was just how far back in the country some of these woods roads went. Around 9:30 p.m., just as it was getting dark, we came to a vehicle parked on the side of the road; a Willies Jeep with a canoe on the roof. We both had a gut feeling that this vehicle belonged to a poacher and we parked up the road out of sight and remained there until daylight. We then walked in a trail for about a mile or so and before long came to a large lake; part of Mint Brook. On the lake there was a boat with two people in it. We observed them for a while but saw nothing out of the ordinary as both were using fly rods. Tired and hungry, we returned to the hotel for a few hours of sleep before our 4 p.m. appointment at the dump.

We arrived at the dump at the scheduled time to find our informant waiting for us. He gave us a complete list of names, vehicle descriptions and areas of poaching. After he departed, Josh and I went over the list. Well, here's a guy who drives a Willies Jeep and carries a green canoe on the roof and he usually leaves home around late evening, drives ten miles or so to a big pond on Mint Brook and sets his salmon nets out for the night. He usually returns home about day-break depending on weather and the number of salmon he caught. We knew this was the very guy we had seen earlier that morning. If only we had known then what we knew now. Returning to the hotel, we had a meal of sandwiches made for an extended stay on the poacher's trail. Returning to the intersection of the TCH and Gambo, we selected an excellent place to park. A contractor was carrying out road work in the area so our vehicle blended in with others belonging to the workers.

At about 8 p.m. who should come up the road but the guy in the Willies Jeep with a green canoe on the roof. We knew we had some time on our hands and we didn't want to spook the suspect by following too closely. Hence, we drove to a telephone booth in Gambo and called the RCMP detachment in Glovertown and explained our situation. He said that his men would not be available to assist until after 2 a.m. unless we had something more specific. You see, we had no means of pulling over a vehicle on the highway, no radio communications, batons or any-thing else to deal with poachers other than our authority, flashlights and a good deal of determina-tion. The RCMP officer said, "Boys, it surprises me that your supervisors would send you out on such an operation without giving you training and equipment to do the job. Don't take any unnecessary chances and call us if you think anything is going down."

We returned to the gravel road and started driving towards where we had seen the Jeep parked earlier. As there were a number of side roads, we decided that, as strangers to this area, it was like looking for a needle in a haystack. We decided to return to the intersection and await for their return to Gambo.

At about 3 a.m. we saw the suspect vehicle come out onto the TCH and turn onto the road leading down to Gambo. With lots of determination but little else, we started down behind the Willies Jeep. About half way through Gambo, they must have gotten suspicious of us as the jeep picked up speed; we did the same. The driver pulled the jeep into a driveway, at record speed and on in behind a bungalow. We temporarily lost sight of the jeep and its occupants. Rounding the corner of the house, we saw two people toss two bags onto a pile of birch junks to which was tied the biggest and most vicious looking German Sheppard I had ever seen. If he breaks the chain that is holding him, which he was desperately trying to do, Josh and I would be mince meat.

Trusting that the chain would hold, we got out to talk to the two men, who demanded to know who we were and why we were chasing them onto private property. Good questions. As there was no way to get to the bags protected behind the dog, and as we had no hard evidence of salmon or nets, we excused ourselves by saying that we thought they were someone else.

As we drove away I said to Josh, "That's the guy we saw on Mint Brook bridge a few days ago." We already knew his name from our informant. Boy this undercover work sure is exciting, tiring and dangerous.

Our informant had indicated that there was a lot of salmon netting going on in Mint Brook and that when some of the guys came home for the weekends, that is where they would go. He indicated that any vehicle you see fifteen miles or so back was most likely being used for poaching; but you need a 4x4 for going that far back.

34

On Saturday morning we decided to return to the hotel, get some sleep and change vehicles. Arriving at the car rental company, we said that we wanted to go fishing well back on Mint Brook and wanted to exchange our vehicle for a 4x4. The guy said that they get people like us all the time and arranged a sturdy 4x4 for us. Great!

With a full tank of gas and a good supply of sandwiches, we left for our patrol on the Mint Brook Road. Taking things easy, we drove for a couple of hours but saw very few people or vehicles. About mid-afternoon we checked a side road and there was indication of fresh vehicle tracks. You could not see more than thirty feet ahead of the truck as the road was grown over with alders.

About two miles down the road, if you could call it a road, we came to the edge of a large lake and there parked was a pickup truck. As there was nowhere else to park, we pulled in directly behind the vehicle blocking its exit. Walking down to the edge of the lake, we could see some footprints leading to a point of land about half a mile away. The walking was easy as the water level was low in the lake leaving lots of shoreline.

Arriving at the point, we could see some people and smoke coming from a campfire over on a point of land about a half mile away. Using our binoculars, we determined that it was two adults and three children. Then Josh said to me, "What's that out on the lake? It's too large for loons." Studying the objects closely, we determined that it was two people up to their chest in water who appeared to be checking a net.

The easy walking was over as we now had to take to the trees to keep from being seen. Arriving within a short distance of the campfire, we soon saw that the two in the water were now with the others by the fire having something to eat.

We had already jotted down the license number of the truck and after adding a few more updates to our notebooks, we proceeded to walk out to where the seven were gathered. As we approached, we could see that a fairly large brook entered the pond here; which must be Mint Brook or one of its tributaries. We weren't really concerned if we were still on Mint Brook or not as netting in any inland waters is illegal.

Upon our advance, there was some nervous glances and low conversation taking place. From this point we could see the plastic floats of the nets in the water. After a brief chat, we both introduced ourselves as fishery officers and proceeded to read the two men their rights. They denied any involvement with netting salmon. After obtaining their identification, place of residence, etc. they said they were leaving to go back home. I told them, "If that's your truck back there you might as well take it easy as our vehicle has it blocked in." At this point in time they were not happy campers but continued back to their truck.

Now the task of getting the two nets to shore. Josh soon solved this by stripping down and physically removed both from the water. Each net was comprised of four inch mesh, about fifty fathoms long and nylon. While Josh was taking in the nets, I started looking around for any salmon that may be hid in the area. Not only did I find salmon, but a small eight foot fiberglass boat, ideal for transporting the salmon and nets back to our vehicle. With a couple of paddles, we made our way with the overloaded boat back to the vehicles. The others had just arrived ahead of us. Now that we had two nets and five salmon in our possession we asked to again speak to the two men, this time in private, away from the children and women.

We told them that they were still under caution and that we had enough evidence to seize their truck after they arrived home. They admitted to the netting but asked that the truck not be seized as it was important for going to work. We agreed and they were later convicted. Along with a hefty fine, the boat, nets and salmon were confiscated and fortified to the crown.

Sunday was a busy day, but that's a story for another time.

The Inshore Draggers

Cape St. Mary's is well known in Otto Kelland's song, *Let Me Fish Off Cape St. Mary's*. It is equally known as one of the best cod fishing areas in Newfoundland. During the days of the schooners and bankers, there was a saying that, "If all else failed, Cape St. Mary's would pay off for all." Probably more to the merchant than the fisher, but that's how it was.

During my career, I had to deal with many conflicts between the fixed gear fishermen and the mobile fishermen, especially in the eighties when fish stocks started to decline and there was great competition for the remaining cod. One such incident comes to mind concerning the inshore dragger operation and inshore fixed gear fishermen. Due to the many problems and complaints, DFO brought in seasonal restrictions that would prohibit dragger operations within six miles from shore.

Cape St. Mary's was one of the areas where a great number of these problems occurred; especially in the fall of the year when a new stock of cod would traditionally come on the grounds. It was at this time of year when inshore fishermen would turn to trawls; using squid or mackerel for baiting hooks. It was also the time of year when the captains and crews of the inshore draggers would make their appearance for an extended period. For this reason, I was assigned a new and very fast boat stationed out of my headquarters in Branch.

I contacted all or most of the captains fishing long-liners and fixed gear, and as most of the boats were fitted with radar, I asked them to carefully document all instances between them and the dragger operations. Such details as distance from land, longitude and latitude, and when possible, date, time, place, and a physical description of the problem dragger should be recorded. At the time, there was a semi-retired long-liner captain living in Point Lance who had a marine band radio and was able to listen in on conversations between the captains of the boats. We all agreed that he would call me if he overheard a problem taking place on the Cape St. Mary's grounds.

It was around mid-September when I got the call from George and his words to me were, "Billy boy, all hell is breaking loose up on the grounds today. A dragger from the West Coast, same one we've had many problems with before, is in among the fixed gear and has already dragged through Denis' trawls. Your brother Freddy and Francis are also having problems with the dragger. Freddy has threatened to go aboard and to have it out man-to-man with the captain." Well, this is exactly the call I was preparing and waiting for.

The weather that day was smooth and calm; ideal for a fast boat. The only problem was that DFO policy stated that we do not go out on boat patrols alone. The nearest fellow fishery officer was in Placentia, an hour's drive away. I then decided, 'What the heck' and went by myself anyway.

As the DFO boat was already gassed up and ready to go, it was only a matter of minutes before I was skimming the surface at about thirty-five knots. I kept in close to the shoreline, in shelter of the high cliffs, to try and avoid detection from the dragger's captain and crew. This worked, as I arrived at the false cape in record time and took up position. I could see the dragger and longliners about four or five miles off. What I was really looking for was St. Mary's Keys' rocks. They are slightly above water and about five miles offshore. The draggers were not allowed inside the six mile limit and thus restricted from dragging down towards Point Lance Rock where the inshore fishermen were fishing with trawls. It wasn't long before I overheard on my radio Captain Denis Nash calling the captain of the dragger to change his course. The reply from the dragger was for Denis to alter course or he would go through the middle of their trawls (again). I thought, "Well now 'Iron Pig' (the nickname of the boat I was using) let's see what you're made of." With that, I hit both throttles and the boat leaped out of the water and the race was on.

At full speed, I approached the dragger. About half way out I noticed a black puff of smoke from the dragger's stack and a change in course. He was pouring on the power as he tried to get outside the six mile limit. They wasted no time getting that drag net on board, but not soon enough for me to positively see it going in over the stern. Arriving alongside of the dragger, I took notice of the fact that he was still in St. Mary's Keys and, therefore, inside the six mile limit. By giving the cut-throat sign, I informed the crew on board of the dragger to cut their engine. This was done, and I asked to speak to the captain. A man came from the wheelhouse and said that he was the captain. I consequently informed him that he was to remain in this area until I had a chance to speak with the captains of the long liners. Failure to do so meant I would see to it that he and his vessel would be arrested and escorted to either Trepassey or Argentia. I also identified myself as a fishery officer, although I was in full fishery uniform. The captain agreed and I proceeded down to speak with the captains of the three longliners in the area.

Pulling alongside Captain Denis Nash's, Captain Francis English's and Captain Fred Roche's longliners, I asked them to fully document what had occurred that day, as well as relating their radar readings to the distance of the dragger from land. I also requested a physical description of the dragger and the comments of their crew members. I informed them that I intended to press charges against the captain of the inshore dragger and that I would be relying heavily on their statements in court. They agreed to do all they could to assist me.

I proceeded back to where the dragger was waiting and they cooperated by taking my tie up line to their boat. I was soon on board and I again asked to speak to the captain. He came forward and after checking his I.D., I informed him of his legal rights which he understood. I briefly told him of the complaints made against him by the other three longliner captains in the intermediate area, as well as my own observations. I told him that charges would be laid against him for fishing inside the six mile limit, as well as less than one mile from previously set fixed gear. I checked the captain's fishing license as well as those of the crew members. There was no problem there. I asked the captain for a statement on his behaviour that day and he said, "I only came inside the limit to see if there were any fish here." "Well," I said "that's not what I or the skippers of the longliners saw." The captain then stated that he had nothing more to say, nor his crew. With that in mind, I left the dragger and returned to each of the three longliners and obtained statements from each of the captains and their crew members. On returning home that evening at a more relaxed speed, I was satisfied that I had all the evidence needed to warrant charges under the Fish Act and Regulations and a better than average chance of success.

Later that fall and winter, a total of three appearances took place before Judge Corbett at Placentia. Testimony was given by all three longliner captains and a well presented case was given by the defence, but the final outcome, guilty as charged. A $1,500 fine and probation for one year was implemented. However, Captain Nash was not compensated for his trawl damage. At the time, $1,500 seemed like a heavy fine, but in retrospect, it was only the price of doing business.

Fisheries patrol in Mosquito Cove, Colinet Island, St. Mary's Bay during mid 1970s. Accompanied by Constable Rick Peacock RCMP who is not shown.

42

The Long Pool

It was that time of year again; soggy south west winds, humid and lots of fog. The salmon were again entering the rivers for their migration upstream but lingering for awhile in the tidal waters to adapt to the fresh and warm water ahead of them.

At about 11 p.m., I decided to make a fishery patrol into the lower Branch river, especially near the tidal waters area as lots of salmon were seen in the gut earlier that day. Driving a mile or so outside the community, I parked the fishery truck and walked down to the river. I began a slow and cautious trek down the main river sometimes called the flats area, and about half way down I came to a pool called 'the long pool.' This was a good place for salmon as this was as far as the tidal waters came in land and a good area for the salmon adapting from their salt water journey to the fresh river.

Constantly stopping and using my trusty binoculars, I scanned the head of the pool. Just at the outer edge of the fog, I thought I detected some movement. I very slowly inched on until I was able to see three people just starting to drag a net down through the pool. Due to the distance and the fog, I was unable to determine who they were. In addition, they were wearing parkas with their hoods up. Hence, I was faced with another dilemma.

By making them aware of my presence, I would no doubt save some salmon still in the pool, but they would disappear into the fog and I would be left to retrieve the net but no poachers. My other choice was to veer off to my left and remain hidden in the fog and in full haste get to the lower end of the pool before they did. I chose the latter as I was sick and tired of dealing with these poachers. A trade off in losing some salmon tonight may pay dividends in the long term if I could get these guys to court and hopefully convince the judge to place them on probation plus a fine.

Being in top physical shape at the time, it didn't take me long to get to the lower end of the pool before they were half way down. The thick fog can work in the warden's favour as well as the poachers. A large tree had washed ashore on the river bank from an earlier flood and I settled in between the branches. From here I could tell that two of the guys were on the opposite side of the river from me and the third guy was still not quite visible. It was at this time that the net became entangled and I could hear them talking about what to do to free it. "Pull on it b'y! Pull on it!" "I am pulling on it but just won't break free!" "You fellows pull on it!" "No use b'y, it won't let go!" "Just a minute," said one of the two, "I'll go over to your side and see if we can break it free. Okay."

He disappeared in the fog briefly and came back walking down river towards me with a bag of salmon hoisted on his back. As the pool was quite deep, he had to pass below me to cross over to my side. Then the second guy said "I'll go over to that side as well." Great, now I can get all three on my side of the river!

The first guy across the river was bent over from the bag of salmon and he was lugging it as he passed within a couple of feet of me. I was able to recognize him and decided to let him pass as I still didn't recognize the guy coming behind with his parker hood tied securely under his chin. He carried a packsack as well, and no doubt, lots of salmon.

As he was about to pass me by, I made my presence known by jumping up and shining my light yelling, "Fishery officer, stop!" The guy with the bag of salmon said, "Cheese," dropped the bag and took off in the fog, no doubt the third guy did the same. Now I was left to deal with this still unknown person just a few feet away and heading back out into the pool at full belt.

As he was weighed down with that bag of salmon, I was determined to get his identity. Splashing across the river, I landed on his back just as he was about to go on shore. A slight struggle developed but I had his identity. Two down and one to go. Taking off the packsack of salmon he was carrying, I told him to leave it where it was and he agreed. Now let's see if I can catch up with the other two as I could hear them going through some trees up a steep hill close by.

Suddenly I noticed that my flashlight was busted as I must have broken it during the struggle. Without a light and with the culprits having such a head start, I decided to return to the net and salmon.

Back at the pool, I waded out and managed to free the net from the large rock it had became entangled in. I released a good number of the live salmon, however, quite a few were already dead or too far gone to swim away. Using the net as a collector bag, I found the other two bags of salmon. With twenty two salmon tightly secured in the net, I dragged the whole works down the river to the causeway bridge where I hid them among the large boulders to pick up later. A satisfactory night's work if I may say so myself.

Twenty one salmon was the tally which I sold with the cheque made out to the Receiver General. One salmon was kept for evidence and charges against the two were laid for netting inland waters. I made an unpleasant remark to the third individual when we next met as I knew he was involved but could not prove it in court. The two accused both entered pleas of guilty and were fined.

Photo courtesy of Don Nash

Lower Branch River. Picture taken by Fishery Guardian Don Nash while on helicopter patrol.

The Missing Horse

It was early September and most of the salmon that had entered Branch River were well up towards the headwaters where there are some great spawning beds of gravel. Consequently, it is also a great attraction for poachers. For that reason, myself and fishery guardians carried out many patrols in the area; sometimes camping up there for a week at a time. It was on one such patrol that a most unusual thing occurred.

It was late one afternoon when we saw four or five people coming in over the hills towards a cabin that was close to the river. One of them was leading a horse that was weighed down with supplies. Unaware of our presence, they settled down for the evening in the cabin. The horse was tethered to a stump. Every so often, one of the guys would come out and check on the horse. At the same time, we were at the other side of the river. Using our binoculars and keeping a close eye on everything that was going on, we realized that these guys were known poachers.

Just before night closed, the horse managed to escape the rope and lost no time in going up over the hill behind the cabin. The horse had just gone out of sight when one of the guys came outside. The alarm was raised and in seconds the men were scurrying around in all directions trying to find the escaped animal.

Bright and early the next morning, we were all up and about. Around 8 a.m., the owner of the horse started walking back out the trail they had come in on. Fishery Guardian Don Nash and myself situated ourselves close to the trail so as to get a real close up view of the guy and maybe intercept him. As he slowly approached our location, we could see that he was carrying a rifle. I said to myself, "There is no hunting season open during this time of year!"

Fishery Guardian Don Nash camped at the "Reef" Branch River in early 1980s.

Photo courtesy of Don Nash

As he was about to pass us, I stood up and said, "Hello!" What a surprised look came on his face as he said, "Uh! Billy, have you seen any sign of my horse? I had him tied on but he got away." I replied, " No, b'y we haven't seen your horse today. By the way, that's a real old looking rifle you have there, a WW1 Lee Enfield, isn't it? Mind if I have a closer look at it?" "Sure," he said. I took the rifle and while examining it, I noticed that the magazine was full of bullets. I unclipped the magazine and put it in my pocket. "What are you doing?" he said. "I'm seizing the rifle as there are no open seasons in this area and also for safety reasons. You will be notified by wildlife officers regarding this matter. "Gosh darn it," he said. "First my horse and now my rifle."

The rifle was turned over to the wildlife officer of the area and the man was charged with carrying a gun out of season in country. He pleaded guilty and was fined. Oh yes, the horse showed up in Branch a day or so later; about twenty miles from the cabin. It was none the worse for wear.

The Sprite Can

It was late July and there had been no rain for a week or more. Salmon were more or less trapped in the pools and avid anglers had given up on fishing as they just weren't taking.

As a rule, I usually completed my weekly reports over the weekend or on Monday morning and then mailed them to my supervisor. On this particular Monday, I was free of the office work around noon and decided to do a foot patrol on the lower section of Branch River.

The day was calm and mild and the flies were out in full force. The walking wasn't so bad as the flies sort of helped carry you along. I checked the pools on the lower two miles or so. There were very few salmon and no anglers to be seen. As I came to an area in the river called the Gooseberry Island, I checked a small sand bar on the footpath. As I saw no fresh footprints, I decided that I was wasting my time up here as nobody with any sense would be on the river today.

As I was about to turn around and go home, I saw something floating down the river. As it passed by I realized that it was a Sprite can. "Well," I said to myself, "there's no wind to blow you into the river and the water level is falling, not rising, so you must have been tossed into the river, and most likely by a poacher." With renewed energy and caution, I began to make my way upriver. I made a careful check at the Salmon Hole, but there was no activity. The next good salmon pools were known as the Darby Pools, and with my ever trusty binoculars, I slowly and cautiously approached the lower pool where I saw a flurry of running about and talking by five people. It did not take me long to determine that they were attempting to jig salmon from the pool. There were two guys on the west side and three guys on the east side, shouting and pointing to the remaining salmon in the pool.

Photo courtesy of Don Nash

Picture of Upper Falls looking downstream. The bottom left shows one of best pools on Branch River.

I quickly jotted down the names of three of the jiggers, but I did not know who the other two were. Since I was still a fair distance below them, I went back down river and crossed over to the eastern side where the strangers were. Carefully making my way up through the trees, I finally came abreast of them. All of them were on the east side by now and they were in the process of packing up and leaving. Convinced that I had seen and heard enough, I walked out of the trees and in their sight. Surprise! Guess who's here?

My immediate task was to get the identification of the two strangers and identify myself to them. I obtained the identification of the two in question, informed all of them of their rights and briefly informed them of what I had seen in the past twenty minutes or so. They were polite and cooperative and when I checked their pack sacks I found two salmon in each; a total of ten in all, each of them with jigger marks. "Well," I said, "there's more than attempted jigging going on here." A quick check of the pool showed only one salmon remaining.

As I seized all ten salmon, the five pack sacks and the five fishing rods, they started to depart and return home. One of the five, came back and said, "Billy b'y, that's an awful heavy load for one person to lug back to Branch. If you want, I will carry some of the load for you." I declined and managed to lug all the seized items home.

Three of the five pleaded guilty on the plea date at Placentia before Judge Barnable. The two I did not recognize at the beginning pleaded not guilty. A trial was set and after hearing the defence and prosecution's account of what had taken place that day on the river, Judge Barnable convicted them of jigging salmon in inland waters. All items of seizure were confiscated by the court and were ordered to be forfeited to the crown. As well, all received a hefty fine. Hence, DO NOT LITTER.

The Warders

*O*t was back in the early seventies and I was still learning the ropes in my new position as a fishery officer. It was late May and the scheduled salmon rivers were still closed to fishing but the commercial fishery for salmon, lobsters and cod was up and going. Consequently, that was where most of our patrols were concentrated.

As I recall, it was around noon when my phone rang and a local resident asked me if the trouting season was open in the Branch River tidal area. I said, "No, not inside the bait and spinner signs which I had posted earlier." "Well," he said, "you should patrol down by the gut area as there is lots of trout fishing going on by a bunch of strangers. They are using spinners and doing well with the trout." As my office was close by the harbour area, I walked down to see what the situation was, taking my badge, I.D. and notebook. Because it was the weekend, I was not in uniform.

Approaching the wharf area, I could see three persons fishing, using spinner fishing rods and one was within a few feet of a posted schedule river sign. As there were some locals in the area, someone must have told the fishers that the warden was coming and all three started to walk back toward a nearby van where another two men were standing. One of the trouters had been in too much of a hurry to reel in his spinner and it was dragging twenty or thirty feet behind him. I put my foot on the line and the spinner was soon imbedded in my boot. The line broke and as all three reached the van, the back door was quickly opened and the three fishing rods were thrown inside.

I removed the spinner from my boot and walked over to the van. All five of them were now hurrying to get inside and to no doubt drive away. I took out my badge and I.D. and introduced myself as Fishery Officer Bill Roche and stated that they were not to drive away until I had spoken to and identified the three who had been fishing. Four of the five men got out of the van and I found myself peering up at four of the biggest men that I had ever seen in one place. The fifth guy in the van was just as big. I also determined that some of them had been drinking and were already half in the bag.

Photo courtesy of Don Nash

Photo of Goose Pond just below the headwaters of Branch River.

Taking out my notebook and putting my foot on

the rear bumper as a knee support for my notebook, I asked all three to show me some identification as I had probable grounds to believe they had been fishing trout during a closed season. It was at this point that the leader of the five told me, in no uncertain terms, what I could do with my badge and notebook. All three observed fishing were now getting very upset and told me that they would not show me any identification. I insisted that unless they showed me their identification that I would see that they were arrested by the RCMP at Placentia as they drove back the Cape Shore road. The community of Branch was a dead end road back then so the only way for them to get back home would have been to go up the Cape Shore.

It was at this point that the leader opened up the rear doors of the van and said to his buddies, "Let's throw this little bastard into the van and take him for a ride and teach him some manners," stating that they were officers of the law with more authority than I. As a couple of them were about to grab hold of me, the guy in the van got out and said, "Stop! We are in enough trouble as it is without you fellows committing an assault!" The fourth guy, who had been silent up to this point, also advised the three not to lay their hands on me. The leader then made some remark towards the other two interveners about how he would deal with them when they got back to work. At this point, all five jumped in the van and sped away.

I hurried back to my office as quickly as possible and called the RCMP at Placentia. Constable Rick Peacock answered the phone and I explained to him what had happened. I also gave him a description of the van, the occupants, as well as the license plate number. He informed me that he would leave immediately to drive out the Cape Shore to intercept them and that I should also drive up to help in the arrest and identification. I also told the Constable how one of them had said that they were also officers of the law. I quickly got changed into my uniform and started out in my fishery vehicle towards Placentia.

At the community of Patrick's Cove, I saw the flashing lights of the police car as well as the van in question. Pulling up alongside, I got out to hear Constable Peacock being told off by the leader as he had done to me. Constable Peacock then asked me if these were the same five that I had seen down by the wharf in Branch and I confirmed that they were. Once again, two of the five were in the van and not giving any trouble.

Constable Peacock, now certain that he had the accused suspects, soon brought matters to order stating that unless they immediately stop resisting myself and the constable and identify themselves like we had asked, that every one of them will be placed under arrest. This was more than what the accused had bargained for, and with a changed attitude, they soon produced full identification and apologized for their behaviour. It took the better part of an hour for Constable Peacock and I to get statements from the five and they were allowed to proceed on their way. One of the two who had intervened on my behalf was sober and allowed to take the van. After they drove away, Rick said to me, "Boy, I wouldn't want to be in their shoes when their boss at the penitentiary finds out about this."

I then returned home and began the task of calling my supervisor Bill Davis at Colinet and doing up the appropriate paperwork on the incident. Later that evening, Bill phoned me back to ask if so and so of the five was to be charged. I said no, as that particular individual was the one who came to my defence during the encounter. Bill said that was very good, as he had since learned that the man's father was in fact a DFO officer and our boss.

After completing all necessary court documentation and setting an appearance date for a plea, a not guilty defence was entered by the three accused and a trial date was set by Judge Corbett.

The accused were represented by a lawyer from St. John's. As I had decided not to call any witnesses to the affair at the wharf site, and since the RCMP officer saw no need to press any charges, the case for the crown rested entirely on my testimony. I was the first to take the stand and it soon became evident that the defence's tactic was to harp on my inexperience on the job. The defence lawyer then started referring to my state of anger during the encounter with the defendants and tried to convince the judge that I had kicked the van after getting angry with the accused. They were referring to when I placed my foot on the bumper of the van while taking notes.

After about two hours on the stand, the defence lawyer still hadn't managed to find any inconsistencies or holes in my statement and began a different strategy of attack. He began to ask me questions on my height, weight, time on the job, etc.

On returning to court in the afternoon, one of the accused took the stand and after being questioned by his lawyer and giving his account of the events, the Crown began its cross-examination. Part of the accused defence was that they did not know they were fishing in a scheduled river and therefore didn't know that they were doing anything illegal. I had taken a picture of the area being fished that same evening and this picture was entered as evidence. The picture clearly showed a number of posted signs, each indicating that this was indeed a scheduled salmon river. After all evidence had been presented, and the crown and defence gave their summations, where the defence went after my credibility once again, the judge, without even leaving the bench, found all three guilty as charged and heavy fines were imposed. He also told the accused that a much heavier sentence would have been imposed if not for the fact that the convicted would have had to deal with an internal review by their supervisors.

The Whittler

It was July and the salmon were making their way back to the spawning beds of the rivers that they were born in some five to seven years earlier. With a survival rate of less than ten percent, they were indeed the lucky ones and would hopefully survive this hazardous run against the legal sports anglers and especially the not so legal jiggers and netters. If they could make it by November, they would reproduce and a new cycle of young salmon would begin. With a little more luck they would survive the harsh winter conditions and return to the ocean in early spring, hopefully coming back again as much larger salmon.

As a fishery officer back in the seventies and eighties, I can say that DFO placed much greater emphasis on inland fishing than compared with today's contracting out.

During the summer months, fishery officers and guardians had a very busy schedule with the commercial and inland fisheries at their peak. It was difficult at times to keep up or even be partly successful in the conservation and protection field. I recall returning home one evening from a long and busy day out on the fishing grounds of Placentia Bay to be called aside at St. Bride's wharf. I was told that four or five well known poachers had left the community on their ATVs to go to their cabin close to the Red Rock area of

Branch river; one of the better salmon pools on that river.

Photo courtesy of Don Nash

Fishery Guardian John O'Rourke with a seized rod at the Upper Falls on Branch River.

Photo courtesy of Don Nash

Fishery Guardian John O'Rourke on patrol at Goose Pond (the headwaters of Branch River).

As the days were longer, I decided in the late evening that Fishery Guardian John O'Rourke and I would go to the falls area of Branch river on our ATV and from there walk up to the Red Rock pool. We arrived at the pool around 9 p.m. and settled in as this was a good time of the evening for poachers; especially for the suspects as their cabin was not all that far away. By 11 p.m. it started to drizzle and fog quickly followed. I had prepared for the weather but unfortunately John had not. By 1:30 a.m. he was chilled to the bone and although he did not complain, I determined we would cancel the surveillance and return home.

Arriving back at the Falls area, we had a hard time finding the ATV, as we had done too good of a job of hiding it away. We finally did locate the machine and arrived home just as daybreak was coming on. We had no need for sleeping pills that morning.

At around 9 a.m. I awoke and my mind immediately went back to the suspects and Red Rock pool. This being Sunday morning, I was hesitant to miss church, however I contacted John and told him to get ready as soon as possible as we were going back to the Red Rock.

Soon after, John and I were on our way back to the Falls and on up the pool at the Red Rock. I was leading and as we were about to go around a bend in the river that would allow us to see the pool, I indicated to John that we should be cautious and quiet in our approach. Stepping into the alders and trees, we slowly rounded the bend and my eyes soon saw a man sitting at the lower end of the pool with his head down. With my trusty binoculars, I determined that he was one of the suspects, and the reason he was looking down was because he was whittling a stick. Instead of doing his job as a lookout to spot the wardens, or anyone else coming up river, he was preoccupied with his pocket knife and piece of drift wood.

We carefully backed off out of sight and hearing distance. I then instructed John to take my binoculars and monitor the lookout man and the area. Due to the alders and vegetation, we couldn't actually see the pool itself.

I proceeded further back down the river to where I could cross over to the other side without being seen by the whittler and possibly others. As the trees on the east side of the river were larger, it was easier for me to approach the pool unobserved. I soon passed by where the lookout was seated and came within sight of the pool. "Well, well ,well, two or more of the suspects pulling on a net!"

As I wanted to get as close as possible before making my presence known, I went a little deeper into the woods and continued on until I was abreast of the pool and the poachers. When I looked out, they were again hauling the net ashore with a couple of salmon inside.

Taking out my notebook, I briefly jotted down the time, place and names of the netters, as I personally knew them all. It was at this time that one of the netters shouted out to a fourth person sitting on the edge of the trees on the west side saying, "Come over and help us clean the salmon!" I think he replied, "I'm on parole you know." "Aw come on over and clean this big salmon," the netter replied. With this the young chap crossed over and they started cleaning the salmon and stowing the net in a bag. At this time all three at the pool had their backs turned to me and I left the trees and walked out to the pool directly behind them. I wish I had a picture to capture the look on their faces as I said, "Well boys, doing a little netting are we?"

No attempt to escape was made by any of them as they knew the jig was up. Soon the whittler joined us and no doubt asked himself, "How did I miss seeing the fishery officer?" We were soon joined by Fishery Guardian John and the process of fully documenting the details and seizure was underway.

After John and I completed our documentation of names, etc., the net, salmon and half bottle of rum was seized as I didn't want anyone getting drunk and in a different frame of mind. The pack sacks and food were left with them as they were a long way from home. At this point the young chap on parole asked me if I could overlook his involvement as he was on probation. I really did not have any evidence of him being involved in the netting, but I wanted him to sweat a little. I informed him I would think about it and I would give him my answer the following day at his home, but in the meantime, the least said about his involvement the better for all concerned. They agreed to this and we went our separate ways. They kept their word.

The young chap consequently was not charged. The other three, including the whittler, pleaded guilty in court and received substantial fines.

You Can't Win Them All

Ernest's Nap

*M*y fellow officers and I of District 2 had been summoned to attend meetings at Marystown to bring us up to date on the ever changing commercial fishery. DFO senior and middle managers were trying to deal with such changes due to the mass decline of cod stocks. It was important that we, as front line fishery officers, be kept informed and hopefully abreast of such changes in policy, quotas, net size, discarding, etc. It was also a great time to meet and socialize with our fellow officers scattered from Cape St. Mary's to Burgeo.

The meeting concluded in mid-afternoon and we were given the choice of driving home or staying overnight until Saturday. I decided that I would leave for home as I had many odds and ends to do around the house. I drove back for Branch that Friday evening and due to the heavy rain, it was after 10 p.m. before I arrived home.

After a light lunch, I was about to retire for the night as I was exhausted after the grueling day and the almost four hour drive in the rain when the phone rang. "Who could be calling at this time in the night?" When I answered the phone, a voice on the other line said, "Hello, you don't know me but I wanted to tell you that there is netting for salmon going on in the river. Four or five of them are going back in again

67

tomorrow. Red Rock area." Then click, the person hung up. Just a few weeks earlier I had passed up on such an anonymous call, only to learn later that it was good information. If I had acted, I would have no doubt nabbed some serious poachers.

As the fishery guardians were finished for the season, I was left to deal with the tip on my own, as I didn't want to call in an officer from Placentia nor was I sure if this call was legit.

The following morning, I arose early. The rain was just about over but everything was wet and soggy. It was hard going, even on the ATV. I unloaded the bike at St. Bride's and started in on a well known and often used trail to Branch River. While heading in the country, I began to ask myself how could someone be netting as there was a huge flood in the river and it was so late in the year. Thinking back to advice I had gotten from retired Warden Michael Campbell, that come mid-August, early September, the poachers put down their rods and nets and take up their guns. Such thoughts were going through my mind as I topped a steep knoll just before getting to some heavy woods called Ernest's Nap. A large number of rocks can be found sticking out of the side of this hill and one had to maneuver the machine in and out to get past them.

Suddenly I noticed something. Topping the hill I came face to face, wheel to wheel, with a guy on a three wheeler ATV whom I knew well. Then up over the hill came another three men on bikes who I also knew.

With the narrow trail being surrounded by the jagged rocks, there was no way to escape. With my bike blocking the trail, I got off and spoke to the boys. They were nervous and I could see that each bike was carrying a heavy load of something. Bags and bags were stacked up on both the front and rear racks of the bikes. As they knew me just as well as I knew them, there was no need for introductions.

After some small talk I said, "Boys, I'm acting on a

Photo courtesy of Don Nash

Picture of "The Buckets" on Branch River. This particular hole is twenty-five feet deep in 'the gorge'.

complaint regarding the netting of salmon on the river and for this reason, I am going to check to see what you have in the bags." They had no objections other than to say that they were not filled with salmon.

I already had a feeling that they weren't carrying salmon, having previously witnessed large amounts of blood seeping out through the bags. However, I had to investigate anyway.

Laying my hands on the bags, I could tell that it was solid meat and no doubt moose quarters. Just to be certain, I opened up a couple of the bags, only to confirm my suspicions.

As I was not a wildlife officer, I informed them that they could continue on but that I would be required to report this matter to my supervisor and most likely to the Wildlife authorities. They agreed that it was embarrassing for all concerned. I continued on to the river just to make sure there wasn't a second bunch of guys in the area. Arriving at the Red Rocks, I found there was too much water for poaching salmon. Oh well, maybe the caller had good intentions as not everyone takes kindly to poaching moose.

The following Monday, I telephoned my immediate supervisor, Derek Rolls at Placentia and informed him of what had taken place on Saturday. He said that he would pass it on to his supervisor Ken Durdle. I don't know if Ken took it further or not, but by noon, the word came down the line that I should do up a report on the whole matter and send it to my supervisor and a copy to Wildlife Officers Hughie Spurrell and Bill Barron. This is exactly what I did and within a day or so, was contacted by Officer Barron. We consequently agreed to meet at a wildlife cabin on the Southeast Road, close to Placentia.

With a pan of porkchops frying in the cabin, I

relayed my story of Saturday's encounter with the moose hunters as Bill and Hughie made notes. They asked me what I thought about getting search warrants and investigating the homes of each suspect. I said that I thought that would be unnecessary, as the guys would not be foolish enough to have illegal meat in their homes after I had told them of my intentions.

The wildlife officers did up the necessary paperwork, and on the strength of my testimony, the issue was set for court at Placentia. As my schedule was somewhat busy with fishery matters, myself and the wildlife officers discussed a suitable date for trial. It was somewhere during these discussions that the trial date set by the judge was somehow misinterpreted by the prosecution.

At 10 a.m. on Wednesday morning, Judge Barnable came to the bench at the courthouse in Placentia. The judge read out the charges and asked the accused to step forward. Once this was done, the judge asked if the prosecution was ready to proceed. Silence filled the courtroom while everyone looked around to see where the prosecutor, wildlife officers and myself were. The prosecution believed the trial to be on a different date. With no prosecution present, Judge Barnable dismissed all charges against the accused. Oh well, you win some, you lose some.

My Faithful Collie

*O*t was early spring and the weather was cold and wet. While sitting at home one evening, I got a telephone call from a young girl in St. Bride's. She informed me of a stray and very sick Collie dog that was roaming around and she asked me if would I go over and help her catch it.

Being a lover of animals, I was soon at the site. With some coaxing and kind words, I soon had a leash on the Collie. It was mutually agreed that I would take the dog and give her a home. A few weeks later and a couple trips to the vet, the Collie was really coming around. We became great friends and because of her gentle nature, I called her Lady.

Well like the flies in summer, so came the salmon and poaching and I was back to the work of outsmarting or being outsmarted. All is fair in love and war.

It was a Sunday afternoon and my scheduled day off. However, by mid-afternoon, I decided to take a walk down to the river to see how things were going. Lady followed me to my gate, but I told her that she must stay. She was disappointed, but obeyed. At least for the time being.

I continued on down a short-cut to the river and upon reaching the bank of the river, I stopped to survey the area. Just then, I saw a bunch of people on ATVs approaching the vicinity. With my binoculars, I

soon determined that these guys needed further surveillance. Quickly darting into the nearby trees, I soon
had myself camouflaged with a good view of a prime
salmon pool. The bikers had arrived and were inspect-
ing the pool with their Polaroid glasses for salmon.
"Well now," I said. "They are in for a surprise if they
try anything here today."

Photo courtesy of Don Nash

Picture taken during flood conditions above 'the gorge' of the Upper Falls on
Branch River.

Well it didn't take very long before their attention
swung from the pool to my direction. I became
uneasy; surely they couldn't see me. By this time some
very obscene gestures and shouts were directed
towards me. "Good God, how can they know I'm
here?" With that, my Collie came up from the bank of
the river right to my hiding place. Oh, if only the
ground opened up, I'd crawl right in it. Well at least
Lady is still my friend.

Fish with Tails

It was early July and the salmon were entering the inland waters for their migration into the spawning grounds. The tidal waters and the Flats area of Branch River were a hang up point for the salmon as they adapted to the fresh water. It was not a particularly good time for fly fishing during this adaptation period and the challenge to the angler was much greater.

While carrying out a patrol on the lower section of Branch River, I came to a pool known as Maurice's Pool, where an out-of-province angler was deeply engaged in trying to entice one of the twenty or so salmon in the pool to take his fly. We chatted for awhile before I checked out his license and tags. During our conversation, he said how it was getting too late for fishing and that he would like to return at first light to try his luck again. However, he said he had been told there was little chance the salmon would be there in the morning as this was a bad area for poachers with nets.

After he had departed for the evening, I walked home a short distance away, and after getting a few sandwiches and a thermos of tea, I returned to the pool with my sleeping bag to settle down for the night.

It soon became calm and foggy and I spent a long and not so comfortable night beside the eastern side of the pool. Coming on daylight the next day, I spotted a lone angler coming up the flats with his fishing rod and singing an old-time song. I knew him well. By the time he reached the pool it was still not quite daylight and as he was on the west side of the river, it was a bit difficult to see just what kind of a hook he was using.

Photo courtesy of Don Nash

Looking upstream at "The Buckets" on Branch River. The river narrows to a matter of feet in this area.

After he had made a couple of flicks and a loud splash when the hook hit the water, I determined that he was using a very large fly. On about his third cast, the hook became entangled in his stocking cap, and in the semi-darkness, he was having a heck of a time trying to get it out. Some less than prayerful expressions were announced, thus I decided at this point to make my presence known and said, "Hey Tommy, when you get that hook out of your cap why don't you head home." "What? What? Who are you? Where are you?" he shouted after I had obviously startled him. "I'm the other Tommy across the river and get out of here before you hook a salmon and I am forced to deal with you in a different way." By this time he recognized me and said, "I'm gone. I'm gone. Thanks." As he disappeared down the Flats he was still singing.

Shortly after daylight, the out-of-province angler arrived at the pool and began his legal attempt to hook a salmon. Not wanting to disturb the pool, I walked some distance below and crossed over to the angler. We chatted as he kept changing flies and used all of his skills to try and hook a fish. Finally, in exasperation, he said, "I bet there is not a damn fish left in this pool after the netters last night." With this he gave up and waded out into the pool to see if the fish were still there. I joined him and not a single salmon was to be seen. "Now," he said. "What did I tell you yesterday evening? I knew they would be netted during the night." "Well," I said, "There are two things I'm going to make you aware of. One is that the pool was not netted as I have spent the entire night here awake and alert. The other being that when we looked at these salmon yesterday evening, each and every one of them had a tail, and they were migrating upstream."

The Retroactive License

It was September and the local inshore fishermen were hoping for a good trawl season. They had removed their nets from the water as this new school of cod on the Cape grounds, for whatever reason, didn't go into gill-nets. It was an especially important fishery, as by this time, fishermen were beginning to clear the decks as it related to their expenses with fish merchants, loan boards, etc. This would be the fishery when one could see some return for one's labour. It was also a higher grade of fish and the cooler temperatures helped to get it to market in top condition and therefore top price.

Cape St. Mary's was traditionally known for a fresh school of fish at this time of year and it was especially known to the inshore dragger captains. Like clockwork, especially in recent years, they anchored themselves on the inshore grounds with little regard for anyone or anything except their own fishing effort.

It was during this season when my supervisors saw it fit to station a small boat out of my headquarters in Branch. I had some luck in dealing with draggers in previous years as daytime operations were aided by the local fishermen. I knew there was a problem again this year as I had received many complaints and I saw the lights of draggers during the night from my vehicle patrols.

A pattern by these inshore dragger captains was to come in on the grounds at night and during stormy days. DFO tried to deal with this by having a large patrol boat stationed at Argentia. The problem with this was that all the radio contact with the Canadian Coast Guard soon alerted any dragger captains inside the six-mile limit. This was the limit set for inshore dragger operations and as it was a two-hour steam to the Cape, one seldom saw a dragger dragging their net inside the limit. It was good prevention and we did have limited success.

It started out a fine morning so, in my twenty-two foot patrol boat, myself along with the inshore fishermen, left port bright and early. I was hoping I might get to the grounds before the draggers moved off. On a good day at full throttle my boat could do about thirty knots but it wasn't fast enough as there were no draggers in the area.

Upon arrival, the fishermen set their trawls and I anchored in a sheltered cove at the False Cape directly inside of St. Mary's Keys which was a favourite spot for cod and the draggers. Some of the best fishing grounds were between the Keys and Point Lance Rock. A mile inside the six-mile limit, the Keys were especially important to me as they were above the high water mark and about five miles off the Cape. A dragger dragging in that area was in clear violation and since I had no radar or other means of determining location at sea, I relied desperately on these rocks.

Shortly after noon, a stiff breeze of wind came on and the inshore fishermen decided to take back their trawls and return to port. Being in a sheltered cove I hung around a while longer. Sure enough, by the time the longliners were fading on the horizon, a dragger started moving in. Within the hour, she was dragging the grounds between the Keys and Point Lance Rock. Unaware of my presence as she returned from the first drag to the Keys, I decided to advance as the loppy sea condition might help cover my approach towards the draggers. Speed was not in my favour due to the rough sea conditions and I really shouldn't have been out there.

About two-thirds out I was spotted by the crew of the dragger, but it was too late for them to get back their net. They headed outward and by the time I got alongside they were under six-miles to land in my estimation. I approached the dragger from the sheltered side and was able to carry on conversation. I asked to speak with the captain, and when he came from the wheelhouse, I identified myself as a fishery officer. I was also in uniform.

I asked the captain if he had a license to drag in the 3L area (St. Mary's Bay) and he stated that he had not. I checked my MASTER license book and found that although he was licensed for 3PS (Placentia Bay), he had no license for the area he was now fishing. I also noted in my book that the dragger was within half a mile or so outside St. Mary's Keys, thus inside the six - mile limit.

Due to the very stormy conditions at this time, I instructed the captain to take his dragger to Argentia where I would do a boarding to further document him, his crew and his boat; it was too rough for a boarding at sea. After some hesitation, he finally agreed to go to Argentia but not before I advised him of more severe consequences if he failed to do so. He retrieved his drag net and started out for Argentia. I left for home in a very rough sea, but with careful maneuvering, arrived safely at Branch.

Bright and early the following morning I was on

the wharf at Argentia. It was raining heavily and there were strong winds from the south—the tide was dead low. Crew on board chose to ignore my presence as I finally managed to get down over the creosote and slimy wharf to the deck of the dragger. Upon entering the wheelhouse and forecastle I asked to speak with the captain. "He's not here," one spoke. When I asked where he was, the response was that he was gone to St. John's, but that he would be back by noon. I then checked the crew's licenses and made notes in my notebook.

As I got ready to depart the boat, I still had that wharf to face. I could see a ladder secured to the top of the superstructure and asked the crew to put it in place for me to climb out. They refused. "Listen to me!" I said. "Put that ladder in place for me to climb out or you will be charged with obstructing an officer in the performance of his duty." The ladder was soon in place.

I kept a constant surveillance on the boat until the captain returned around noon. I again boarded the boat and asked the captain to show me his vessel registration and licenses. He produced them with a sarcastic grin on his face. Upon checking his groundfish license, I could see that the license had been changed to permit him to fish in 3L. Not only was it changed but also back-dated beyond the previous day and signed by one of the senior managers in the regional office of DFO. I was left angry inside but without further recourse.

After departing the boat, I immediately contacted my supervisor and apprised him of the situation. He too was upset at the retro-active license, but by the time my complaint got to middle management, it was losing steam. A day or two later I was told to drop the matter but that the situation would not happen again. You win some, you lose some, and as a junior civil servant, you don't rock the boat too often.

The DFO lawyer decided against charging the captain with fishing inside the six-mile limit. I was told that I was not likely to win considering I had no radar or other electronic gear on board for positioning and, that in my estimation, there was only about half a mile in difference when I arrived alongside. There was the captain, his crew and radar to say they were outside the six-mile limit.

I often wonder if the persuaded senior bureaucratic civil servant understands the hardships they can cause to others by a simple stroke of the pen. I sincerely doubt it.

The Case that Never Was

During the years 1982 to 1984, numerous complaints were being received from Grand Bank, Arnold's Cove and St. John's DFO offices about illegal fishing for scallop in the Presque area. The suspected poaching was being done by the captain and crew of a longliner (which I shall not name). Although our licensing records indicated that the captain had a license to fish scallop in inner Placentia Bay by means of scallop drag, the complaints stated that a diver was doing most of the scallop harvesting; a practice that was illegal under the Fisheries Act and Regulations. Attempts had been made to monitor this particular vessel and crew but no firm evidence was obtained to support the charge.

On October 2, 1984, I was asked by my superiors to try and determine what was going on in the Presque area regarding these complaints. I started my first patrol from Arnold's Cove on October 2nd on board the fisheries patrol boat *Badger Bay*; commanded by Captain George Brown and crew. We proceeded to Isle-A-Valen where we determined it to be a good hide-away location for the fishery's vessel while I carried out my land patrols. Over the next few days, the captain and crew would land me at St. Leonard's, a short distance from Isle-A-Valen, and I would walk over to St. Kyran's, overlooking Presque Harbour. The

82

day of October 3rd was miserable with a strong easterly wind and drizzle. I spent a long and wet day observing the suspect longliner but no activity or fishing took place. I consequently, returned to St. Leonard's and was picked up by the *Badger Bay* and spent a comfortable night in Isle-A-Valen.

Early the next morning, I again got landed in St. Leonard's and walked overland to St. Kyran's. As I approached St. Kyran's, I could hear the loud noise of a compressor on board the longliner. I located the vessel about half way between St. Kyran's and the government wharf. Using my binoculars, I determined that a diver was in the water and a deck hand shucking scallops. Due to the distance involved, I decided to try and get a closer view. Following what used to be a main roadway in that once prosperous community, I was slowed by overgrowth of alders and trees, and by the time I arrived at the site, I saw only five bags of scallops being hauled on board. The anchor was then lifted and the suspected longliner set out towards the far end of Presque into Beckford Cove. I determined at this time that I did not have enough evidence to lay charges for illegal scallop fishing.

With the weekend approaching, I called Captain Brown on my radio and asked him to pick me up at St. Leonard's. We proceeded back to Arnold's Cove as we knew from complaints and our surveillance that the longliner returned to the Marystown area on Friday and unloaded his scallop catch for the week. He was a resident of Kilbride.

The following Monday, Fishery Officer Derek Rolls and I departed Arnold's Cove on the *Badger Bay* along with Captain Brown and his crew. Again using Isle-A-Valen as a tie up area, Derek and I spent many uncomfortable hours hiking, trying to keep a close eye on our suspect, as the vessel continued with its scallop fishing. Due to the constant moving of the suspected vessel, it was decided that Officer Rolls would spend more time aboard the fishery vessel in case I needed their assistance while I scurried along over-grown trails from Presque, St. Kyran's and St. Anne's.

I still had no luck in obtaining solid evidence to warrant a charge. Finally, out of exasperation, Officer Rolls boarded the longliner on October 11th and told the captain of our suspicions and that if he continued, there was a good chance his fishing and diving gear would be seized if charges were laid. To this the captain replied that he was only diving to determine where suitable mussel farming areas were located as he intended to farm there in the near future. I continued to remain an unknown observer.

On the third week of my surveillance, I was again working alone in the Presque area. We left Arnold's Cove on the 15th of October and again tied up at Isle-A-Valen. On the morning of October 16th, I once again got landed at St. Leonard's and walked overland to St. Kyran's. As I approached St. Kyran's, I heard that familiar noise of the compressor on board the vessel. It was music to my ears and I knew they were back to their old tricks. I vowed then and there, "If you want to play cat and mouse games, so will I!"

I arrived at the site where the suspected longliner was anchored which was just a short distance from the church in St. Kyran's. It was positioned in a secluded cove that would not allow a longliner and scallop drag room to maneuver in a legal operation and thus ensuring plentiful scallops for a diving operation. I arrived within sight, and approximately 100 feet away from the vessel, I could observe all its activity. I was fully convinced that the occupants on board were the same two that Officer Rolls had warned the week before. There was one thing nagging me. The deckhand on board looked awfully familiar to me. Where had I seen him before?

At approximately 9 a.m., the captain of the longliner donned his diving suit and went over the side, assisted by his crew member. An empty orange coloured bag, made of dragger twine, was given to the diver. Approximately fifteen minutes later, the diver returned to the surface with a full bag of scallops. The deckhand would then take the bag and give the diver another. He would go under again and within another fifteen minutes, returned to the surface with another bag full. The second bag was green coloured. I carefully noted everything in my notebook.

After watching this operation for about two and a half hours, I decided that I had all the evidence I needed to lay charges against the captain and crew of the suspected vessel.

Since I had no means of boarding the longliner, I then decided to return to St. Leonard's. On my radio, I instructed the captain of the fisheries patrol boat to proceed from Isle-A-Valen to Presque Harbour to intercept and detain our suspected vessel and to pick me up at the government wharf for further investigation.

Returning to St. Kyran's, I again did surveillance on the vessel as I awaited the arrival of the patrol boat. As soon as the patrol boat entered Presque Harbour, she was spotted by a crew member. Consequently a great flurry of activity took place as the compressor hoses were detached, scallop bags were placed over the side and the anchor was pulled up. After getting underway and out from the government wharf, the scallop bags were released to the bottom. As the two vessels came abreast of each other, Captain Brown of the patrol vessel informed the captain that he was to remain where he was while he continued to shore to pick up another fishery officer.

After the patrol boat had picked me up, we proceeded back to where the longliner was waiting. As I was the only fishery officer on board, I asked Captain Brown for the assistance of a crew member in case I needed help in seizing equipment, etc. Captain Brown obliged, and myself and the cook, Randy Williams went on board. After identifying myself and Mr. Williams, I then read the captain and crew of the longliner their rights and asked for their identification. I recalled who the familiar face was, as he was one of the two charged back in 1982 for fishing trawls in a restricted area of Renew's Rock and the brother-in-law of a very important person with DFO. If this wasn't enough, the captain of the vessel stated that he too was a brother-in-law of this DFO senior official. Undeterred, I briefly explained my surveillance of the longliner and the crew and the captain's actions over the past few weeks and in particular, their actions of this day.

I consequently proceeded to seize the air hose from the compressor, the wet suit, air tanks, etc. I itemized each piece of equipment on a sheet of paper and had the accused initial it. They were both informed that charges would be laid. With that in mind, we departed the vessel and returned to Arnold's Cove. On the way back, we didn't have any champagne, but we did have a great steak dinner thanks to Captain Brown and Randy.

Now the paperwork. After securing all the seized items in my basement at my home in Branch, I proceeded to write up a full report of the time spent on this one case and its end result. I then faxed my report to my supervisor in Placentia. Within hours my phone rang and my field supervisor told me that I was to proceed to the Grand Bank office the following day for further discussion on the matter.

Arriving at our district office around 2 p.m., there was concern over my report on the activities of the captain and crew of the suspected longliner. The area manager wasted no time in calling myself, the district officer and the sub-district supervisor into his office. Photocopies of my report were held by each present and the area manager instructed the district officer to read it aloud. After this was done, he asked each of us what we thought of the possibility of a successful outcome, reminding us all that the DFO had just come through a very public and high profile case. Thus he regarded that serious consideration should be given to laying charges against one of our director's brothers-in-laws, especially as one of them had already been charged and convicted just two years earlier.

To this, the district officer and the sub-district supervisor stated that my case as presented was one of the better cases they had ever seen brought forth and that the chances of a conviction in this matter were as good as they get. Knowing our area manager as I did, I knew that his next statement to all present in the room must have been very difficult and that the pressure from above must have been great. He instructed us that no further discussion or the laying of charges was to take place without his specific approval. I returned to my office in Branch somewhat confused.

As luck would have it, I was advised to attend a six week law enforcement training course at the Royal Canadian Mounted Police Academy in Regina and was obligated to leave the following day. At Regina, my days were filled with training and classroom duties and I had little time to recall on the Presque affair.

Upon returning home in December, I went down to my basement and low and behold, all the seized items were gone. Asking my mother what had happened to the items during my six week absence, she stated that a fishery officer had been instructed by his supervisor to take back the seized items and return them to the captain of the longliner. When I questioned my superiors about the reasoning and legality of removing the seized items without my approval, I was met with vague and not so vague answers. Unfortunately that is where the case remains to this day.

The Greasy Wharf

It was mid-summer and the trout in the Branch gut harbour area were big and plentiful. The local fish plant was in full operation and the filleting of fish left lots of morsels to be washed out into the gut area by the freshwater discharge chute. This was a favourite place for the trout to gather as they fed on the discards of the filleting knives. It was also a great attraction for the poachers hoping to get their hands on these large trout.

The wharf was constructed of treated timber; some pieces as large as 12x12 inches. Where they came together made an ideal place to hide in comfort beneath the concrete deck while using fish hearts as bait on a hand held string. There was plenty of room to sit, place your can of hearts down beside you and catch huge sea trout. Of course, upon the deck of the wharf was your other half who would keep an eye out for the warden.

It was again the daily routine of the wardens and the poachers—trying to outwit each other. I seized lots of fish, hooks and strings but very few individuals as they would not be fishing by the time I got there. The grin on their faces told the whole story. What could you do? I would however get my revenge.

One afternoon I made a check at the wharf area and as I walked out on the deck, a couple of local chaps came over to me and said, "You should have been here a short while ago. One of the boys went down beneath the wharf and before long was back up covered in grease. Every stitch on him was ruined. He cursed you up to the clouds. He blames you for greasing the whalers and beams." Well now, isn't that too bad.

Later, towards the end of the month, I submitted my monthly gas and other expense report to my supervisor Derek Rolls. He called me one day after reviewing my expense sheet noting that I had purchased two tubes of grease at the local gas station. He had previously heard of the greasy wharf incident and said, "Now I wonder what use you had for the grease?" "Fishery officer provisions," I noted.

The Transfer at Sea

The inshore crab fishery had been open for a couple of weeks in both Placentia and St. Mary's Bay. When the quota was about to be reached, the word came down from DFO that the crab fishery in Area 10, (St. Mary's Bay) would close at 6 p.m. the following day and that no crab could be landed after that time. I, along with other fishery officers in the area, went out to the various wharfs and communities to inform the fishermen, especially the captains, of the upcoming closure.

While over at the wharf in St. Bride's, I met with one of the fishing captains who had just off loaded his crab from Area 10. When I informed him of the closure, he stated that he had baited crab pots in the area but that he had no intention of going out fishing crab the next day. He also said that if DFO informed him yesterday, he would have taken in his pots today instead of baiting them. I informed him that these were my instructions and that the landing of crab would be illegal after 6 p.m. tomorrow. With his coat under his arm, he mumbled something or another, got in his truck and drove away. I made an entry in my note book on our discussion.

The morning following the closure, I was catching up on some office work at my headquarters when the phone rang. A representative of the local Fishermen's

Committee had been asked to contact me to see if I could get permission from DFO to allow this captain, the one I had spoken with two days earlier, to land his crab as he already had fifty boxes or so stacked below deck. I informed the caller to give me an hour or so as I would have to contact my superiors for an answer. This I did, and within half hour, the word came back down that no extension would be given for the landing of crab from Area 10 and that the crab fishery was officially closed. Failure to abide by this closure would result in charges for fishing crab during a closed season.

I immediately contacted the Union representative and informed him of the Department's decision and the repercussions of the landing of crab from Area 10. Shortly after, I was again called by the Union representative saying radio contact had been made with the captain in question and that he informed them to tell me that he intended to land his crab at Point Lance wharf later that afternoon regardless of the closure.

As this was a direct challenge to DFO and their mandate to regulate the fishery, I called my immediate supervisor Derek Rolls at the Placentia office and apprised him of the situation. It was decided that we would go to the wharf at Point Lance to await the crab boat and two other officers would monitor the wharf at St. Bride's. Within an hour and a half, we were in place at the landing sites. Late that afternoon, Derek and I saw a boat coming in from Area 10 towards us. As the weather was clear, smooth and calm, we could see her approach while still a few miles away. As the boat drew closer and using binoculars, we determined that it was the boat in question. Something happened then that gave us a problem later in court. We both made entries in our notebooks as to the time, date and place, but there was a discrepancy of twenty minutes or so. Was it because one of us made an entry while the boat was still well offshore while the other made the reference when she was close to land?

Parked in the DFO truck overlooking Point Lance wharf and cove, we were no doubt very visible to the approaching captain and crew on board the longliner. When they arrived within about a mile or so of the wharf, they made a sudden change in course and the longliner was now heading towards Cape St. Mary's and no doubt St. Bride's. We waited around for awhile in case they changed course again as we knew it would take them much longer to reach St. Bride's than for us to drive. Besides there were already two officers over there. A local resident then came by to say that the captain had called him and asked him to inform us that he was off loading at St. Bride's.

Radio contact was made to the officers at St. Bride's and they were updated on the events of the crab boat. Arriving at St. Bride's, we informed the two officers there that they could return to their headquarters as the overtime was tight and the day was getting on.

An hour or so later, the suspect longliner entered the harbour and everything that wasn't bolted down was stacked on top of the hatch leading to the fish hole. After securing alongside, Derek and I boarded and spoke with the captain, advised him of his rights, and, indicating that he understood his rights, we asked him if he had any crab on board from Area 10. To this he replied, "I don't know, you'll have to check the hole yourselves to find out." Not wanting to create any unnecessary tension as a large crowd of fishermen now occupied the wharf, Derek and I started removing all the objects stacked on the hatch. We were not very particular where or how the items landed.

Finally, we got the hatch open and not so much as a crab leg was to be found. The captain refused to give a statement or any further comments and with nothing left to investigate, we returned home.

About an hour later, my phone rang and the caller told me that we had gotten the wool pulled over our eyes. I was informed that a longliner fishing crab in Area 11, Placentia Bay, had just entered port loaded down below and above the deck even in the forecastle and that the word around was that a transfer at sea between the suspect longliner from Area 10 and the longliner from Area 11 had taken place. I immediately left for St. Bride's wharf. Arriving a short time later, the crew just began off loading the longliner as a truck was waiting for their catch. One of the first things that grabbed my attention was the large amount of crab on board and that almost all the crab on deck were belly up. This was not normal in the stacking of crab. I spoke with the captain and members of his crew on the large catch as well the stacking and was told that they had never seen so much crab in their pots before. They also said that the boat started getting so crowded for space that they were forced to dump them in a pile on deck. The driver of the truck indicated to me that he would have to check with his boss as he suspected a lot of the crab on deck were dead. The captain later told me that the buyer would take them only on the condition of open receipt and a determination would be made at the plant as to quality. I made entries in my notebook about all this, including a description of the truck, license plate number and fish company as I could not determine if any laws under the Fisheries Act and Regulations had been broken. I then returned to my headquarters convinced but unable to prove a transfer at sea had taken place.

At approximately 10:30 p.m. my phone rang and I knew I was speaking with a reputable informant regarding the crab landings that day. The caller said that he had overheard a conversation on just what had taken place. He also told me that crab from Area 10 had been put on board the longliner fishing Area 11. I gave my word of confidentiality not to involve him and I called Sub-District Supervisor Ken Durdle at his home in Marystown and told him of this latest development. Ken gave me the approval to get another fishery officer and locate the crab truck carrying the illegal crab. I consequently called Fishery Officer Anslem Griffiths of Ship Harbor and he agreed to assist me. Anslem was waiting for me at the office in Placentia and we started out on our search. At around 4 a.m. that morning, we found the truck parked outside the fish plant at Trouty; crab still on board.

We quickly called the manager of the fish plant, and before long, both our boss, Ken and the manager arrived. We then called in a fishery inspector to get his experienced opinion on comparing the state of the crab from Area 10, as they were among the first loaded onto the truck, and the remaining crab from Area 11, which had been properly stowed in boxes below deck.

By mid-morning, just about all of the suspect crab were dead. The plant manager indicated he would not be paying the fisherman in question for the dead crab. Some consolation. The suspect crab were seized until there was a further investigation on the matter, and a receipt was obtained to Receiver General.

The following day, I contacted the two captains as well as all crew members but none agreed to give a statement or comment on the matter other than to deny it. Fishery Officers Rolls, Griffiths, Durdle and I did up our reports on the matter and we presented it to our Prosecutor Mr. Gordan McNab. After reading over our reports and with further discussion with Assistant Prosecutor Ann Fagan, they agreed we should proceed with charging the captain with fishing in Area 10 and if successful in court, we could later charge the other captain with an offence under the Fisheries and Oceans Act and criminal code. The prosecutor also told us that under oath the accused would be asked to tell just what took place on board their boats that day.

A date was set for a plea and a not guilty submission was entered by the accused. A trial date was set by Judge Barnable at Placentia and we all gathered that afternoon to try and sort out the matter. The accused was represented by a well known lawyer, one I had dealt with before.

I was the first called to the stand and quizzed about the events of the day in question. I referred to my notebook on a number of occasions regarding time, place, etc. It was the defence's position to prove that not enough time had lapsed from when the longliner changed course off Point Lance wharf and her arrival at St. Bride's to off load fifty boxes or so of crab to another boat. I was also quizzed on the distance between Point Lance Cove and St. Bride's. I made an error here, as most of my previous patrols of the area were done in boats less than twenty-two feet. I had no electronic equipment on board to accurately measure the distance from Point A to Point B. I estimated ten to twelve miles, but later testimony by a witness called by the defence stated it was actually more like fourteen to fifteen miles. Thinking back on it afterwards, I should have broken the distance down to shoreline points and heads as I knew each and every one well .

I then would have come up with approximately the same figure as the defence. Oh well.

When Fishery Officer Rolls was called to the stand, he also referred to his notebook on a number of points. It was here that a discrepancy was discovered between my notes and his. There was a twenty minute difference between when I recorded the actions of the longliner off Point Lance and Fishery Officer Rolls' entry. Was it because I made an earlier entry than Fishery Officer Rolls or was there a problem with one of our watches? I'll never know.

For whatever reason, the Judge went with Fishery Officer Rolls' entry as being the most accurate. Evidence was also entered to the state of the crab on the upper deck, implying that they were taken from the water earlier. Questions were also asked to why the crab in the fish hold were in better shape than those on top and why were most of them all stacked bottom up?

The accused captain did not take the stand on his own behalf. The crown called four of the six summoned witnesses who all denied, under oath, that a transfer had taken place at sea. Two were not called as the judge and prosecutor agreed that there was no point in calling them as this case was like flogging a dead horse.

After all was said and done, Judge Barnable declared the accused not guilty as he felt not enough time had elapsed between the time we saw the longliner off Point Lance and its arrival at St. Bride's. Knowing the calm and smooth sea conditions that day, he thought it would take eight able bodied men quite a bit of time to transfer fifty or so boxes of crab from the fish hole of one longliner to the deck of another secured alongside. However, I knew that dumping such boxes of previously properly stacked crab explained why most were belly up. But that's the law. You can't win them all.

The captain from Area 11 was later paid for the seized crab. However, it was much less than the legal fees involved no doubt.

Whistle On the Night

It was late June and the salmon were starting their yearly return to the rivers. Most of them are returning for the first time since leaving as smolt a year or more ago. For some of the lucky ones, it is their second excursion, but rarely is there a third time as the mortality rate is high. First they have to survive their juvenile years in the rivers and brooks, then at sea while they grow into mature two or three pound salmon and then the perilous return trip along the coastline from maybe as far away as Greenland to the river they left as smolt.

Well, the ones returning to Branch River also had the odds stacked against them from day one and it was no different now on their return. In spite of the best efforts of DFO and conservation and protection officers like myself, the poachers were bound and determined to intercept them when and wherever possible by whatever means.

As was usually the case at this time of the year, our workload as fishery officers was exceptionally heavy and hectic, in spite of incentives given by DFO such as overtime, professional training, equipment, as well as benefits extended to our hard working fishery guardians in their seasonal employment.

It was a calm and foggy evening and I was totally beaten out and decided that was one night when the salmon are going to have to fend for themselves as far as I was concerned. With this in mind, I retired to bed early, but for some reason, I noted that the tide would be low later that night and it would be a good time to put out a net underneath the causeway bridge. However, it was very difficult to keep a net there due to strong currents that would occur during rising and falling tides.

My subconscious must have gotten the best of me because I slept solidly until 1 a.m., but when I awoke I knew my sleep for that night was over. Getting up and checking the weather, it was the same as it had been earlier; calm and foggy. All you needed to make soup out of the fog was some salt and pepper.

After a cup of tea, I started out to walk to the causeway bridge, which was about a ten minute walk from my house. I kept to the shaded areas away from the street lights in the community as I didn't want my presence to be noticed.

As I approached the bridge from the west end of the causeway, someone gave out a single, but loud whistle. Ah, the lookout was warning the netters. I broke into as fast of a run as my short legs could manage towards the bridge. Arriving there, I shone my four-celled flashlight down onto the water. There, on the eastern side of the bridge, I saw two suspicious looking people. I had a good idea who they were, but without seeing their faces, I still couldn't be sure.

I swept my light into the centre of the channel and there, struggling up to his chest in the water, was a third person. I shouted for him to remain on the eastern side of the bridge and that I was a fishery officer. However it fell on deaf ears. He finally made it to the shore but just before getting lost in the fog. Nevertheless, he made the fatal mistake of looking back at me and my four-celled flashlight. It was a familiar face indeed and no stranger to poaching.

Due to the very thick fog, there was no point in chasing them as there were too many directions for them to go. I went down over the causeway and up under the bridge, where at low tide, a small sand and gravel bar are above water. There, I saw lots of fresh footprints and a rope leading from an abutment into the water. It was exactly what I had expected to find.

Pulling on the rope, a discarded commercial gillnet started to come out of the water along with four salmon; one very large. I managed to release three, but the fourth was dead. I secured the net and salmon a short distance away and decided to wait and see if the poachers would attempt to return home using the causeway. Half an hour, an hour, an hour and a half, and finally through the fog and silent night, I could hear the sound of water logged socks and boots approaching from the east.

With my ever trusty Mag Lite, I shone it directly into their faces as they came abreast of me. One I had seen and identified earlier that night, the others I put the spotlight on and in a very rough and angry voice was told by one of them, "Get that *#%$^& light out of my face," to which I replied, "I'll get the #$%^&* light out of your face when I have identified you."

With their hoods up and because of the fog, I still wasn't completely sure who the other two were. With that they ran off the causeway and went down onto the flats of lower Branch River. With the fog, I did not pursue. Instead I secured the net and salmon in my basement and went back to bed about daylight. Not a bad night's work for someone who was tired to the bone.

The following day, I went over to the house of one

of the suspects—the individual who was hidden by the fog. He lived alone and his table was covered with empty beer bottles. Consequently, he was hungover and was not in a good mood. I read him his rights and advised him to his right to legal aid; he understood. I subsequently asked him for a statement about what had taken place last night, and while his answer didn't surprise me it did upset me.

As the man crossed his thumbs and swore on his mother and father's grave, he told me he was not netting the river last night. I knew that I would not get a statement from him as he was a hardened poacher.

Before leaving his house I said to him, "It's one thing to net the river for salmon, another thing to refuse to give me a statement, but it is unforgivable for you to bring your dead parents into a bare faced lie as you and I know it to be." As I left his house his head was hanging.

Charges of netting salmon in inland waters were laid against the one person whom I did identify, and he was convicted. The whistler and his companions got away; but I still know who you are.

Stakeout at the Red Rock

*B*ack in the late seventies and eighties, it was not unusual for the DFO to apply for and get money to hire senior high school students as seasonal fishery guardians to help out with the heavy work load of regular staff. These young students were given a badge and power of enforcement under the Fisheries Act without any real training in law, conservation or protection for a crash course and on the job experience. Although unskilled, they were dedicated and were of great assistance on the rivers during the salmon run.

Photo courtesy of Don Nash

Picture of Upper Falls on Branch River during flood conditions.

For one reason or other, I was usually one of the lucky wardens to get one and sometimes two of these students. Such was the summer of 1978 and 1979, when Raphael Roche and Pat Nicks were hired to assist me and the regular guardians in our inland patrols. They were strong, sturdy and dependable young men who were sometimes taxed to their limit by my demands of night and day patrols over sometimes rugged conditions and terrain.

One such incident comes to mind when I decided to take them both patrolling at the Red Rock Pool on Branch River. As an excellent pool for salmon it also attracted the dedicated and the not so dedicated poacher. I did have a concern with all illegal fishing, but especially the hard core poachers and for this reason, it was extremely important to keep our presence and tent location unknown to all persons in the area. One of the great deterrents to poaching is in having people know the wardens are out on patrol. Exactly where was the question.

The previous year I had set up tent in the same area except on the eastern side of the river where the ground was more level. However, the site was discovered as that was the side of the river anglers and poachers used to get around the pools in their trek further upstream. As the west side was more suitable for mountain goats than humans; yeah, you guessed it. That's where I decided to set our tent on this particular stakeout. Anyone who has ever gone camping knows that if a tent isn't set on level ground, it is very uncomfortable, especially at night. Three people trying to sleep at night on sloped terrain means you go to bed on the higher side and wake up on the lower side; maybe with someone's foot stuck in your face or ribs. As I said, the boys were dedicated but I know I was pushing them to their limit and I guess a few comments were made outside my presence.

After setting up tent, we cut a short trail to within a few feet of the river bank. This would allow us to go for water or check for people without showing ourselves. Our tent was close enough to the pool to hear people talking, noises, etc. I had cautioned Pat and Raphael to approach the pools carefully and to be extra cautious if a known poacher was in the area.

On the morning of the third night, it was Raphael's turn to go for water. Although we were living out of can food, water was still needed for washing and tea. Pat and I were getting things squared away from what represented a tornado from the previous night when it dawned on me that Raphael was gone longer that usual. Slowly and cautiously I went out to investigate his location. Low and behold I found him sitting and chatting with a young angler whom I knew had a low resistance to foul hooking.

Raphael returned shortly and we had breakfast in silence. I was not a happy camper as our cover had been blown. They weren't happy either but maybe for different reasons. Anyhow, I gave the order to pack up everything and we would return home at once. On the walk back, I led the way as usual. I sometimes wonder about what the boys' thoughts and whispers were about. Fair to say, every cloud has a silver lining.

PS: When I asked Raphael why he was talking to the angler, he said, "I forgot to look before stepping out onto the river." Understandable.

Special People

Special Memories

Between Your Ears

*O*t was May 24th weekend and for once the weather was cooperating as it was sunny and not too cold. As the trout season was opening up for non-scheduled waters, there would be lots of anglers out and about for that great outdoor holiday. My supervisor had asked me to work that weekend and carry out some inland patrols on the Cape Shore, Placentia, Colinet and Branch areas. At this busy time, it was important to help keep a check on illegal fishing in scheduled waters; especially for young smolt salmon now migrating to the salt water for their first time, as well as to check anglers for daily bag and possession limits.

On Saturday afternoon, I was driving along the road between Branch and North Harbour, and in a large pit close to the Little Barasway River, I saw a dozen or so people around a large fire cooking up a scrumptious meal of salt beef and cabbage. Slowing down but not wanting to intrude, I was about to continue on when someone in the crowd shouted out, "Come in Roche you old fart. Are we too good for you or what?"

Knowing it was said in humour, I drove into the site and started chatting with those gathered around. A few ales were being consumed and that dinner in the pot sure smelled good. They were indeed a very happy and joyful bunch; some of them I knew quite well.

Having enjoyed my visit, I was about to get up and leave when I saw a person coming out through the low growth of trees between us and the nearby pond. He was carrying a broken fishing rod, an open trout basket and it was easy to tell that he had more than a few beers in him. When he finally emerged from the bushes, I was looking at a man who stood at least 6'4", with shoulders that would span a yardstick. He came directly towards me and growled, "What the devil are you doing here?" "Oh," I said, "Just checking with some friends and insuring that no illegal fishing was going on."

Photo courtesy of Don Nash

Denis Nash at "The Buckets" Branch River 2001.

I could see by the open basket that he only had two small trout. To this he did not take kindly and drawing himself to his full stature, he again glared down at me and said, "Now what the bloody hell could a little guy like you do to someone like me if I were breaking the law?" To which I replied, "Well that's a bridge I would have to cross if and when I came to it." All around the campfire was quiet at this time. He said back to me, "Why the hell would the Department of Fisheries and Oceans hire someone like you over someone like me?" I replied, "Probably because of what one's got between the ears, not what's below them." There was dead silence for a second, until someone started to laugh and before long we all joined in; including Mr. 6'4".

My Uncle's Point of View

*O*t was that time of year when the commercial and the sport fisheries were at their peak. Like the commercial fishermen and sportsmen, the fishery officer was extra busy trying to keep a presence at the many wharves and rivers—an impossible job at the best of times, but made somewhat achievable by the ever faithful seasonal fishery guardians. And we must not forget, the poachers also had their sleeves rolled up ready and watching for every opportunity to get around the rules and regulations of conservation and protection. Or simply put, outsmart the wardens.

In my role of fishery officer, like many others, I was working extra long hours and still found there were patrols and things that just didn't get completed. It was just such an occasion when I was returning home from a river patrol where the poacher had the last laugh. Upon entering my home, Uncle Stephen was paying a visit to my parents and he, like my parents quietly listened to my ranting frustrations about the demands of the job and the luck of the poachers. After a quick lunch that evening, I was still in a bad mood when my uncle decided to give me some good advice; keeping in mind that my uncle was born some seventy years earlier. He was more or less of the opinion that poaching wasn't always wrong as it was sometimes accepted as a rightful means to put food on the table.

As I was about to depart the house, Uncle Steve

112

said, "Billy, sit down for a minute." "Uncle Steve, I'm in too much of a hurry to sit." With a straight forefinger and firm voice, he repeated, "Sit down." I agreed and sat close by him. "Now," he said, "Think about this. Suppose you were flat broke and there was not a jingle in your pocket. You knew a friend or relative who would like to have a salmon to eat and along with that, things like cotton balls were in your mouth telling you how good a cold beer would taste. Now imagine that someone came along as you sat on the corner fence and said there was a school of salmon in the long pool just waiting to be netted and I know someone who will pay us two dollars each for them. If you were put in that position, what would you do?" "Thanks, Uncle Steve. Good night." I consequently went off to bed thinking about what my uncle had said.

My Old Man

$\mathcal{G}$rowing up in rural Newfoundland with a father who was both a fisherman and hunter, as well as two older brothers, one easily practiced the traditional ways. Being the youngest of three brothers, we started hunting and fishing in our early teens—each one learning from our seniors, Grandfather, Father, Uncle, Brother, friends and neighbours. One of the highlights of the day was the retelling of the day's activities. This would be done after supper in a lamp lit kitchen heated by a wood stove; there was no television. The topic most discussed was the negative parts regarding our day's hunt. Perhaps it was the covey of partridge or ducks we or the dog scared off or how we completely missed them with our single or double action guns.

It was during one such discussion with our father that we were interrupting each other to tell Dad about the bad offer we made and, Dad being the patient and a good listener, waited until we had told and retold each disappointing event, even though we had had a fairly good day overall. As silence finally befell, Dad spoke his thoughts on the day's event as told by us. "Boys," he said, "you had a good day hunting, but you seem to dwell on the negative. You see, we can't have things one hundred percent our way. If we did, greed would rule the hunt and there would be little or nothing to hunt over time. The law of nature says there should be escapement. The other lesson in these so-

114

called bad offers is a very important part of our learning." This was one lesson I never forgot.

On Retrospect

It was the early seventies and I, as a new fishery officer was about to take my first helicopter ride with veteran Fishery Officer George Furey. We agreed that we would meet the pilot at our warehouse in Colinet.

It was about 10 a.m. on a May morning when we started our coastal and inland patrols. We travelled from Colinet to Cape St. Mary's, checking on salmon nets, lobster fishing and draggers. From the Cape, we would fly inland and check all scheduled rivers, along with any beaver dams that may be obstructing the young salmon on their journey to the ocean.

Shortly after leaving Colinet, I began to notice colour changes on the ocean shoreline waters; a lime green and creamy colour. Out in the John's Pond area, there were miles of these colours along the shoreline. Through my headset, I said to Mr. Furey, "What's causing the colour changes in the water?" To which he replied, "Billy my boy, don't you know what's causing that?" "No sir, I don't," I said. "Billy, that's millions and millions of herring spawning. These are some of the best spawning areas for herring in all of Newfoundland. It is also one of the best fishing areas for herring in the world."

I think back so often on all the great advice he gave me as he truly was a man of great knowledge. As a WWII Navy veteran with a great appreciation towards the lifestyles in rural Newfoundland, he understood the need to adapt one's lifestyle towards responsible actions and respect for our resources.

It was some years later, as Mr. Furey had since retired, when my supervisor, Bill Davis and I were monitoring the herring seiners in the Mount Carmel section of St. Mary's Bay. Dozens and dozens of huge seiners, with their huge nets, were cleaning up on the spawning herring. It was load and go, all day and night by seiners from all over the province. As we sat in our fishery vehicle, in our green and brass-buttoned uniform, out on Mount Carmel Point, an elderly gentleman came down from his house overlooking the area. A bunch of seiners were within a stone's throw of the shoreline; each with its fish holes and nets full.

Coming up to our vehicle the elderly man said, "In the name of God officers, surely people with your authority and understanding can put a stop to the slaughter and destruction of our herring stocks. If this is allowed to continue we will see the loss of our herring forever." I wish I could remember the gentlemen's name as he had a great understanding of what was really happening. We were part of the government that sanctioned it in the first place. His words did come true in that by the early eighties, the herring had become so scarce that it was difficult to get a few to bait your lobster pots, or a few to salt for the winter. The herring are now slowly recovering, but in the many helicopter patrols I have made over that area in later years, never again did I see those coloured waters.

Squaring Off

$\mathcal{I}$t was September month and Fishery Guardians Don Nash and John O'Rourke and I were alternating in camping in on the upper waters of Branch River as that was where most of the salmon were now concentrated. It was important to maintain such patrols as Branch River runs sort of parallel with Route 100 along the Cape Shore, and therefore only a couple hour's ride from any community along the way. I believe these well known poachers fail to fully understand the devastation they have caused to this rapidly declining fish species and possibly even its extinction. It's wrong to say that, "I may as well get my share as so and so is getting his." Two wrongs never make a right.

I had just relieved Don and John at a tent site we had set up at the Buckets, where the Burnt Hill River enters Branch River; a well known gathering place for the salmon and therefore poachers. There is a large, flat area on the Burnt Hill River just before it flows into Branch River which is covered in green vegetation and attracts many moose and caribou. I had just finished settling in and decided to go to a knoll overlooking both rivers as it was such a fine and peaceful evening. I soon noticed a large moose with a magnificent set of antlers peacefully feeding on the flat. He was indeed an extraordinary animal and I enjoyed just sitting there watching him.

After a short while, I also became aware of another

movement in the grass not that far off. Getting out my trusty binoculars, I soon discovered it was a lynx. The huge cat must have been six feet from nose to tail and slowly and cautiously it crept towards the moose. To watch this lynx move, one could easily understand and appreciate the stealth and power these equally magnificent animals possess in the food chain. But surely to God the lynx wouldn't take on such a powerful animal as this moose!

Slowly but surely the lynx was closing the distance between it and the moose until it was about one hundred feet away from its potential prey. It was at this time that the moose became aware of the danger, and started looking around the tall grass as it let out a few powerful snorts and began shaking its head. Still the lynx continued with its cautious approach, now at about fifty feet from its target.

Finally the moose spotted the lynx, faced him and began to stomp his hooves, heaving out loud snorts as it smashed its powerful antlers through the surrounding brush. Now that it had been spotted, the lynx rose to his fill stature and began to slowly circle the moose—as the moose began to circle the lynx. "Boy, they are squaring off," I thought, and I had a ringside seat to a fight that had probably never been witnessed by a human eye.

The challenge between these two great animals lasted ten minutes or so without either making a charge to attack. It appeared the lynx was trying to get behind the moose, but the great animal would have none of that. Finally the lynx decided to break off the attack, and slowly moved back up the side of the river and out of sight. The moose crossed to the far side of the river and slowly disappeared up over the nearby hillside.

Billy Roche on headwater patrol and camping on Branch River, 1970s. Accompanied by Constables Rick Peacock and Art Doody of RCMP.

Note: The author didn't agree with ATV use in environmentally sensitive areas but stressed that it was necessary in order to keep up with the poachers.

As night was closing, I returned to my tent and boiled the kettle on my propane stove and enjoyed a light snack as I thought about what I had witnessed. Usually when camping we only lit a single candle so as not to announce our presence to whomever might come by. However, on this particular night I decided to break the rule as I was about half way through reading Cassie Brown's book *Death on the Ice*. Turning on my flashlight, I angled it to shine on the pages of the novel, and while I became deeply engrossed in this great tale, another most unusual event occurred. A huge bird, most likely an owl, began hovering and clawing at the tent. It was a startling moment as these wings and claws seemed powerful enough to carry both myself and the tent away. I extinguished the flashlight and the bird went on. Putting down my book, I made an entry in my journal under the light of

the candle—of one of the most unforgettable nights of
my life.

Fishery Guardian Don Nash camped near Branch River in early 1990's.

The Blessed Salmon License

It was back in the seventies and the commercial salmon fishing was in full swing. To have a salmon license as part of your fishing enterprise was indeed a lucky break as it meant an almost immediate cash pay-out for your day's catch.

One such fisherman was Mike Burke of Long Harbour, Placentia Bay. Mr. Burke was a well known and respected fisherman of the area in spite of a hunting accident some years earlier in which he lost his arm to a shotgun blast. However, his spirit never daunted and he continued to fish and provide for his wife and children. But, Burke was again faced with a deadly obstacle. He developed cancer and when he could no longer remain up and about, he was forced to remain at home in bed. His faith in God and especially Saint Ann never faltered. A picture of Blessed Saint Ann was always close by on his bed stand.

It was the time for the renewal of all commercial salmon licenses, and I being the fishery officer for his area, was summoned by his family to stop by his house as he was very concerned about having his license renewed. This I did and after chatting with Burke in his room, did the necessary paperwork and renewed the salmon license. Upon my completion of the license, Burke placed it on his bed stand and I departed.

The following morning Father Pomroy, the Parish

priest, stopped in to see Burke as was his daily custom. Upon entering the room, he soon noticed that Burke was not quite his usual happy manner in spite of his illness. "Well Mr. Burke," said Father Pomroy, "how are you today?" "Oh, not so good Father Pomroy. I'm afraid I did a great disservice to Saint Ann last night." "Oh," said Father Pomroy, "Now whatever could that be, since you and Saint Ann are such close friends?" "Well Father, it's like this. Yesterday the fishery officer came by and issued me my salmon license, and after he left, I placed it on the stand next to my bed. During the night, I was feeling sick and from time to time, I would reach out in the darkness for Saint Ann's picture to bless myself with while I prayed to her. Well Father, when daylight cleared away, I discovered I had been blessing myself all night with the salmon license. Do you think Saint Ann will understand?" "Mr. Burke," said Father Pomroy, "your deep faith in Saint Ann and your religion will more than compensate you for the mistake. I would even venture to say that Saint Ann and the Good Lord, like ourselves, have a good sense of humour and I feel that under the circumstances, Saint Ann will award you with added benefits." To this, Burke was greatly relieved and joined the priest in a chuckle over the matter.

A Measure of Friendship

For the first half of my career as a fishery officer, I had the good fortune to work with a remarkable conservation officer named Michael Campbell. We did countless day and night patrols together. Michael wasn't keen on taking people to court for minor conservation offences. However that is not to say that he wasn't dedicated. Day or night, rain or shine, Michael was out there as a conservation and protection warden. He was respected by all, even the poacher.

One of our favourite patrols together was camping out, sometimes for a week at a time, in the back country and headwaters of the salmon and trout rivers. He was a great story teller, and with close to thirty years on the job, he had many stories to tell. But to me he was more than that; he was a mentor.

I recall one time not long after my appointment as fishery officer. As we sat in our tent cooking up a meal of salt beef and vegetables, I was telling him about this person that I thought he knew. He listened and when I finished, he quietly said to me, "How well do you think you really know this person?" "I believe I know him well," I replied. "Maybe so," Michael said. "But one measure of really getting to know a person is by sitting down and eating a barrel of flour with them." Michael obviously knew him better than I did.

The next time I met this person, I took Michael's advice and ate a meal with him. Needless to say, I didn't like him very much after we were done. Michael's suggestion was certainly a lesson learned.

A Legend

Legendary Fishery Officer, Arthur O'Keefe of Southeast, Placentia, served with DFO for over forty years. He was one of the first people to ride a bicycle out the Cape Shore while carrying out his duties of coastal and inland patrols. Back in the forties, bicycles were a rarity in parts of rural Newfoundland, with some of the residents never having seen one.

While driving through the community of St. Bride's, an elderly lady was out in the yard picking up wood chips. When she looked up, she saw Arthur in his full brass button uniform drive by on his bike. Rushing into the house, the elderly women said to her husband, "I just saw the devil on a swivel pass down the road!"

Arthur, being one who enjoyed a good yarn and laugh, used to get a great kick out of telling and hearing that story. As a new green-horn officer back in the early seventies, I had the great luck and privilege of being trained by, and working with, officers like Arthur O'Keefe.

Author's Note

As a federal civil servant, I kept hearing goverment managers telling me how one must see the big picture. Well I believe that was once true, but in recent years, with all the government cutbacks, the big picture is not what it used to be. Looking at the big picture now means looking at the bottom line—in other words focusing on the 'savings line'—saving money but not saving our resources.

THE BRANCH RIVER SONG

Here's a little tune
Called the Branch River Song
Not all that many verses
It won't detain you long

We'll start on the causeway
In the month of July
You'll see silvery salmon by the score
Eager for the fly

Up around the long hole
It is beautiful and wide
With schools of salmon coming in
On each and every tide

Then around the turn
You'll see the Otter Rub my by's
Fish the head of this lovely pool
If you want to get a rise

(CHORUS)

Oh they're there from Branch and Paradise
St. John's and Corner Brook
Braggin' about their favourite fly
Comparin' every hook
Some will go home lucky
With a salmon in the bag
A few will go home cursin' sayin'
"I forgot to bring me tag"

A half a mile later
You're in the Salmon Hole my friend
You'll forget about the dozen chores
To which you must attend

Move on up a little bit
You're in the Darby Bow sure now
Try the strain in the upper hole
There'll be salmon there I allow

Three miles above that famous pool
And then you're in the falls
The Upper and Lower
Between two granite walls

Then up to peaceful Red Rock
Three deep and lovely pools
Watch out for Shannahan Wardens by's
And go by to the rules

(CHORUS)

Seven or eight pools later
You're in the Buckets at last
From the lower end, eastern side
Try your luck at a cast

Around a few more tired turns
You're in the Reef my boy
What a spot to pitch a tent
In the latter end of July

At the head of this winding river
You will finally spy a pond
Named for the hundreds of Canada geese
That once lay there upon

The beauty that will surround you sure
It can compare to none
Take care of Branch River by's
It'll be there for your son

(CHORUS)

I don't think I detained you
All that very long
Now I hope you have it
The Branch River Song

Donald Nash
Branch River Warden
(1978 - Present)